Deep and Simple Wisdom

Also by Ma Jaya Sati Bhagavati:

The 11 Karmic Spaces:
Choosing Freedom from the Patterns That Bind You

First Breath, Last Breath:
Practices to Quiet the Mind and Open the Heart

Deep and Simple Wisdom

Spiritual Teachings of Ma Jaya Sati Bhagavati

Kashi Publishing
Sebastian, Florida

Published by Kashi Publishing
11155 Roseland Road
Sebastian, Florida 32958

Edited by Devadatta Kali
Cover and Book Design by Laurie Douglas
Cover Photograph by Swami Dhumavati
Back Cover Photograph of Ma Jaya by JPI Studios
Photograph of Neem Karoli Baba by Ramgiri Braun

Printed in the United States of America

ISBN-10: 0-9838228-5-9
ISBN-13: 978-0-9838228-5-1

Neem Karoli Baba
Ma's Guru

Be like a mountain peak
looking toward the endless blue sky.

Be filled with the wonder of the day,
and like a mountain, let no one's anger
move you from your tranquil heart.

Let no anger of your own arise
and cast its ruinous shadow,
but let the day take its natural course
and flow with the sureness of love.

Be wise and meddle in no one's affairs,
lest you jump into another's chaos.

And always have a sense of humor
to bring laughter to the day,
for anger has no place in your life.

Like a mountain, rise high above it.

Contents

CONTENTS

About Ma's Teachings

"Love, serve, and don't judge." Five short words, no more than the sum of the thumb and fingers of either hand, but words that contain enough advice for a lifetime well lived. They are the essence of Ma Jaya Sati Bhagavati's spiritual teaching, and in the pages that follow you will come across them time and again.

Sometimes the profoundest wisdom speaks in the simplest way.

That also is the essence of Ma's teaching. She presents the age-old truths that form the core of every religion on earth, with special emphasis on the often difficult, hidden teachings of Shaiva-Shakta Tantra. Yet you would not know that you were listening to what great Hindu holy men and women have taught for thousands of years; this is because Ma speaks the language of ordinary life today. Sometimes she even speaks the language of the streets. It's all about reaching those most in need and bringing them the message that they matter, that their lives matter, and that it matters what they do with their lives.

"Love yourself first," Ma also says. "If you do not love yourself, how can you love another? Love God, and love to love God." God for Ma, and for the whole of Hindu tradition behind her, is both Mother and Father—Shakti, the feminine creative power, and Shiva, the pure consciousness of one's own being. They are one and inseparable from each other, and from each one of us.

"Know yourself, know the beauty that is in you." Another of Ma's often repeated teachings, this one is about the spiritual quest for Self-knowledge, for recognizing that each person, no matter how exalted or lowly, is one with that same divine Self that we call God. Everyone is divine, and the purpose of life is to discover that.

For Ma and her students, that is not the end of the story, though. Life does not end with enlightenment, but a new life begins. Here Ma cautions her students that finding God in oneself is not enough. In India that would be like finding a stash of delicious mangoes and then eating them all in secret. We are not to be secret mango-eaters. For Ma the best way to enjoy God is not merely to sit in the quiet of meditation, but to emerge from that bliss and actively worship God through service to others—by feeding the hungry, caring for the ill, or going out to the homeless on the streets and recognizing that the same God who shines from our eyes shines from theirs as well. When every action becomes sanctified through selflessness, life becomes truly fulfilled.

Spirituality is all about love. Not the self-centered, romantic love that finds us constantly clamoring for attention and creating expectations that set us up for the agony of disappointment. True love has no expectations. It is unconditional, because it mirrors the unconditional love of God.

This love is the golden cord on which the pearls of Ma's wisdom are strung. At one end of the cord is love for God, which in the end is self-knowledge; at the other end is love for each other, which expresses itself in service. When the ends are joined and a garland is formed, we have the perfect unity of spiritual practice, which consists of *jnana* (knowledge), *bhakti* (devotion), and *karma* (action)—the classic Indian paths to Self-realization. How easily and naturally Ma integrates them into a single way of being for those who live by her words.

As for not judging, this vital way of thinking is closely tied to Ma's interfaith practice. Ma, a Jew who has experienced Christ and honors the gods, goddesses, prophets, and saints of all religions, teaches an open-hearted—and open-minded—message of acceptance. Early on in Ma's spiritual awakening, Christ appeared to her and instructed, "Teach all ways, for all ways are mine." She has never forgotten that simple message. In Christ or Krishna, Allah or Yahweh, Ma sees one and the same God.

Her broad spirit of acceptance applies not only to the many forms of God, but also to God's children. As Ma declares repeatedly, "There are no throw-away people." We are to regard everyone as our brothers and sisters, regardless of race, ethnicity, religion, sex, gender, or sexual orientation. As children of God, all human beings are worthy, and all are welcome in Ma's interfaith embrace.

Ma constantly tells us to be in our hearts, and in all probability the word *heart* is her most often used word after *love*. By *heart* she does not mean the physical organ that pumps blood through our bodies as long as we live and breathe. She does not even mean the heart as the seat of our feelings. In the Tantric sense, *heart* is our deepest consciousness, which is the pure center of reality. It is this heart of awareness deep in each one of us that is the light of God.

Breath is another of Ma's frequently used words. Physical breath is the sign that we are alive in the body; the spiritual breath that Ma teaches us to cultivate awakens us to the life of the spirit. We learn to live in oneness with the universe, with each other, with ourselves, and with the God within that is our Self.

Every religious and spiritual tradition on earth has its holy men and women, and among those spiritually awakened souls, a few are distinguished as great teachers. The messages of all great spiritual teachers have one feature in common, and that is their universality. At the deepest level there is no contradiction from one to another. All teach the sublime message of unity, that God is one and we are all one in God. Depending on the tradition, the teacher is known by various names, but by whatever name, the genuine spiritual preceptor is empowered to teach. The Russian Orthodox tradition calls such a preceptor *starets*, the mystically inclined Jewish sects use the term *rebbe*, Zen Buddhism confers the title *roshi*, and Sufi sects honor their spiritual guides with the term *shaykh*. In the Hindu and Sikh traditions and that of the Kargyupa sect of Tibetan Buddhism, the favored title is *guru*.

To be a guru is to have a divine calling and a divine commission. The term *guru* denotes a teacher empowered by the experience of God—one who has become a channel to conduct others to the same experience. A guru is also a link in a chain of spiritual tradition, for in Indian religions, and in others as well, the deepest teaching is transmitted personally.

Ma's own guru is Neem Karoli Baba, who was well known throughout India for decades before being "discovered" by young Westerners in the 1960s. Ma took Baba's transmission and passed it to her own students. She also gave it to those who were already committed to other traditions, and more importantly she gave it to those who cared little for the terminology and trappings of religious life.

The teachings contained in this book come from Ma's *Morning Pujas and Prayers*, her daily e-mail postings that allowed her to be a constant presence in the lives of her *chelas*, or disciples, around the world. A full year's worth of teachings went into the making of the book. Some of the original, unedited postings are short, filling no more than half a page; others are longer, running to as many as three pages. Some center on a single topic, and others deal with several. Some are specific and others general. What all of them have in common is their spontaneity. In their original form they are the outpouring of Ma's in-the-moment thoughts on spiritual life, lovingly intended to inspire and guide her students.

For many readers the best way to approach this material will be to read one short section at a time, perhaps as part of a morning or evening meditation. This comes closest to the experience of those who found Ma's teachings in their in-boxes every day. It also allows the reader to engage more fully and to become aware of the deeper meaning of each teaching.

To create a book out of Ma's spontaneous teachings, the daily postings first had to be sorted by subject matter. After repetitions were removed, they were combined into larger pieces, each with a predominant theme. The edited pieces then seemed to fall naturally into four groups, which form the book's four main sections. Each section stands alone, yet functions within a larger structure. Part 1 is an invitation to spiritual life. Part 2 deals with the many pain-bearing obstacles and challenges that a spiritual aspirant must overcome. After this acknowledgement that we all experience some forms of negativity in the habitual conduct of our lives, Part 3 focuses on the positive ways to neutralize them and to direct ourselves toward greater purpose and fulfillment. Part 4 is mainly concerned with the fruits of spiritual practice and the transformation of life from the ordinary into the extraordinary.

A secondary structure emerges in the book's three interludes, entitled "Shiva Ratri," "The Mother," and "Durga Puja." Because the pieces that make up the main body of the teaching represent a year's worth of Ma's thoughts, it seemed fitting to give a sense of the year's cycle as well. The interlude entitled "Shiva Ratri" evokes the annual springtime celebration that commemorates the grace of God the Father in granting enlightenment to those who sincerely call upon him. Of all the pieces in the book, it gives the truest feeling of what it is like to be in Ma's physical presence, face-to-face with the power of her eloquence. By the same token,

Durga Puja, the great autumn festival of God the Mother, is the subject of an interlude that occurs later in the book, creating a sense of symmetry and balance, much like the mighty pillars of a suspension bridge. Because much of Ma's teaching revolves around the feminine aspect of God, it seemed only fitting to place at the very heart of the book an interlude entitled "The Divine Mother." This consists of four pieces, each devoted to one of her countless forms: Durga, Kali, Ganga, and Shakti.

Although providing variety, this secondary structure does not interrupt the main trajectory of the unfolding spiritual journey but serves to remind us that throughout that journey there is a spiritual support on which we can always depend. The simple truth is that there is no failure in spiritual life. We need only make the effort to succeed, and God's grace will see to the rest.

In the pages that follow, you are invited to begin a journey like no other, the spiritual journey into the heart of your being. Ma calls this "the ride of a lifetime." Get ready, and know that an incredible adventure lies ahead.

Devadatta Kali
Editor

PART ONE
The Beginning

An Invitation

When you begin your spiritual journey, you may not realize that you and your life will never be the same again. Spiritual life is all about change, so get ready for the ride of a lifetime. If you do not change, you stagnate, and stagnation is truly a small, steady death of the heart.

Meditate on your life as it is this day and see what you have a desire to change. You are the architect of your own destiny.

Start by ridding yourself of that which you do not need. So many of you are attached to your pains and sadness. The mind so often thinks of the glass as half empty, but the heart will call you to think of the glass as half full. By being in your heart, you can transform your mind from being always negative to being always positive. You can pick yourself up from the darkest moment. It is only your perception that changes, but with it everything else changes, too.

Do not imprison yourself in the limitations of fear, but challenge yourself and feel your own strength. It is easy to follow the same old patterns of fear, over and over without thinking, never getting out of the darkness. Do not underestimate yourself to yourself again. You can train your mind to take a new, deep look at all the old paths you are used to following. When you have a full and awakened heart, you can attain knowledge from all that has hurt you in the past.

Choose now to follow a path of light. When you have something beautiful, loving, and God-filled to express and you suddenly want to hold back out of fear, then you must know that you are following an old habit. Keep on going, and you will reach a point of loving yourself and not being afraid.

Even as you begin to feel the spirit of God, memories of fear may come up. Say to yourself that you will not sabotage this moment. Not any more! This time you shall devour your life instead of letting your life devour you.

As you walk closer to God, new thoughts arise in your heart, and these heart-thoughts will keep you on the spiritual path. There are thousands of subconscious thoughts inside of you. An ego-thought that comes from the mind can make you unhappy, yet the heart can take that same thought, transform it, and change you into a happier person.

Each day make for yourself a silent time, and become the observer of your emotions. Most human beings do not know how to be alone with themselves and remain distracted by the outside world. As you go deeper and deeper within, you get into the habit of not paying much attention to outside stimulations. The outer distractions of your life will disappear as you become gradually detached from concerns over their outcomes.

When attachments begin to melt away, you will recognize that somehow an inner wisdom is at work, a subtle energy that is there all the time.

That is because your spirit is full and perfect. You may be accustomed to being in touch only with your mind, but now you are in touch with the spirit. It is just a matter of learning how to listen. As you listen, you learn that you are a child of God. She, the Mother, is the source of higher wisdom within you. Listen to her voice, which beckons you on and on. Being present in every moment, you will find that first and foremost you are a spiritual and loving being.

You will become strong in your love for God and for the guru, your spiritual teacher who guides you toward God. Every one of us has the ability to develop our God-energy to its fullest. This shakti, this spiritual power, is the deepest and wisest part of our being. In your awakening spiritual life, search your heart for the limitless love that you and God know exists there.

Because the oneness of God lives deep within your being, the key to happiness is in your own heart. Your heart is a transmitter of all the wisdom of the ages. New answers are really old solutions. They have always been there; you just have never been quiet enough to hear them before. Remember, it is the mind that dissects the heart and sabotages your moment of awareness. Be in your heart always, be aware of the divine presence, and let all the God-answers surface and bring you joy. They will quiet the ordinary mind and make it your God-mind. In the quiet of this God-mind you can learn to be happy even if you do not have control over outer events. The joy of the spirit is right there, an invisible force that flows through your being. With it you can create your own miracles of love and joy.

These will be miracles for others also, and that is the beauty of loving God. When you seek happiness for the hearts of others, happiness will not elude you. In serving others, you are being served. What the Mother loves the most is when you are aware of the feelings of others, so abandon your fears of rejection, and love without wondering if you are going to be loved in return. Do not hesitate. The great beauty of this spiritual path is that you just cannot get it wrong. Keep focused on love, and send it out whenever you can. This will bring you to your own divinity. Surrender to your own greatness, and know that this greatness is God's love.

As your breath naturally flows in and out, let your life flow, knowing in the deepest part of your being that it is rooted in God. Light up each day with thoughts of love, and do not be afraid to nourish your mind with kind thoughts toward all whom you meet. Breathe in and out as deeply as you can. As your lungs fill up, know that you are loved, and as the breath goes out, know that you have a great ability to send out love.

God is touching you this moment. Your guru is protecting you this moment. God and guru give value to each moment of life. There is no need to be separate from God the Mother or God the Father, not even for a split second.

Leave the prison of your mind, and be in your heart always. You can do this. You can break through all your boundaries and let every cell in your body become enchanted with God.

What bliss awaits you in finding that your God is always with you! Take away the light of God and you have nothing. Walk toward that great light and you bow to your own existence. Your innermost Self is all knowledge and wisdom. The Self is the light and the joy of God and Goddess. Eternity and infinity are merged together in you. "Thou art That" is the ancient teaching. Know you are That.

Knowledge Is Empowerment

Is there any reason in the world why you would want to give your mind power over you? It breaks my heart to think of anyone who is crippled with attachments, bad habits, indulgence in instant gratification, darkness, or thoughts of revenge. Negativity turns on the one who allows it in and brings bitterness and old age so much ahead of time. People who are so afflicted remain alone in life and die alone. This does not need to be.

How easily you can lessen your vital energy, your shakti, by wasting time or being petty or hurting others. Does it really bring you happiness to do these things? Say to yourself, "I am not this mind; I am the Mother's shakti." Repeating this will bring you to a greater awareness of who you are—in your heart and not in your mind. Your mind can give you only illusion, your heart can bring you truth.

Be ever watchful, and whenever possible take a few minutes to detach yourself from your mind and enter into the reality of your heart.

The mind dulls the eyes, but the eyes of one who lives in the heart dance with the reality of God the Mother and God the Father. In God's great dance of life you will at first feel yearning and seeking. Yes, even as you are dancing with God, you are seeking, because the mind will not let you understand that God could be so close as to dance with a mere human. Yet God and Goddess dance not only with humans, but with all of creation. Enter into the freedom of your God-heart and knowingly, joyfully, join in the dance.

Once you have gained some rule over your mind, you can dive into the heart's pool of nectar and direct your shakti upward toward the thousand-petaled lotus at the crown of the head, where all the answers to all questions live.

Remember always that the Mother is the central force. She is your shakti. She will eat all your regrets, doubts, confusions, and fears, all your pettiness and jealousy. She will take away whatever keeps you from knowing the beauty of your true Self. She is your Mother and you are her child, and even though she adores you as you are this moment, if you want to change, she will help you with her great, upward flow of shakti.

The Mother is the ocean of goodness and compassion. Ask the Mother anything at all. The Mother is listening to all prayers and will answer them in her own way. Just call out to her, and whatever your path is, she will come to you in a form you can understand.

The Mother is the pure essence of love and intuitive wisdom. She will teach you of the great freedom from darkness and bring you into the light. She is your personal goddess who is with you with every breath. Call on her now and ask her to bring you her divine grace. Do not be afraid that what you want is too small or too big. The Mother is always a breath away and wants to know what your greatest desires are. She will let you know down to your bones how much you are loved and adored by God the Mother and God the Father.

Misery can never touch those who call on the Mother in any of her forms. Bow to the Mother within the heart whenever you can during this day and every day of your life. Get into this wonderful, calming habit of acknowledging the Mother within. After a while she will make herself known and remind you of your own devotion. What a grand path you can be on if you remember to be grateful for your life!

You were born to realize the Self. Why not start this very moment?

The true goal of life is to return to the source of all power within your being. In fact, life in this body of flesh is a great opportunity provided by the Mother for her children to evolve into herself. Life can be a magnificent journey from ignorance to wisdom and from pain to spiritual bliss. Life is all about love, and spiritual life is all about love and service.

When sorrow hits your heart, know that you are surrounded by the love of the Mother. It will get you through the sorrow. If you feel unworthy, give up your feelings of unworthiness and come to the realization how much God loves you. If you do not lead a spiritual life, if you are negative, or if you are passing rumors about others, you are crippling your heart and keeping yourself away from the healthy joy of loving God.

To overcome your problems you need only turn to the Mother in any of her many forms. No matter how you think of your god or goddess, she will help you to rid yourself of negative imaginings and fears. Call on her by any name and ask that she take away whatever stands in the way. If you just *ask*, she will make you more receptive to all the good in life—and strong enough to handle that which is negative.

Asking for these boons will make you more flexible and much freer in how you live. You will become much more relaxed, even in your spiritual practice, and nothing will seem impossible. You will be able to accomplish anything and everything. Ideas begin to arise, not from your ego but from your heart. You begin to feel in harmony with the divine will and thus in harmony with the universe, not separate from it or at odds with it.

Through the breath you can attune yourself to God the Mother and feel her loving arms around you, sustaining and nourishing you. As you tune into the Mother's loving heart, all pettiness begins to drop away. Do not try to hold on to anything, but let it go. As you cast aside all thoughts of smallness and negativity, know that you are not limited in the eyes of the Mother. Do not limit yourself in your own eyes.

You have an immense power within yourself, a reservoir of shakti. Through your own great and wonderful thoughts of God, you can discover a universe of good will within your heart. Develop the power of that will by being disciplined. Meditate every day until meditation becomes your second nature. Meditate and feel the love that is your birthright. You will find yourself discarding all that is dark and small and negative as you ride the wave of light back to the Self within.

Be devoted to God, because, in truth, nothing can destroy the *bhakta's* devotion. Nothing can weaken the capacity for love in the devotee's heart. There are no limitations on the spiritual path. The *jivatman*, the individual soul, is in every one of us, and this soul is connected to the universal Self. We are all one, and God the Mother loves when we know that in the depth of our being. Remember, God alone is real.

Seeking Satisfaction and Serenity

Eventually you come to a point when you realize that nothing of the world can satisfy you. Everyone is fighting for a little bit of the world when in truth everyone wants a whole lot of God. On any given day, all around you, people are seeking some type of pleasure or possession. The mind keeps saying, "More, more, more!"

But at the same time the heart asks, "More of what?" After a while you begin to think that there must be a better setup than what you have right now. Then the realization that you're just running from God comes over you, and you begin to thirst for her presence in your life. At this point the best thing to do is to let all worldly desires lose their impact upon your thoughts and feelings. Want God and God alone.

When the mind is able to give up delusion, it turns to the reality of the God-heart and the pure understanding of God's light that is inside you. You can feel it now. Look up toward your third eye and see the light between the eyebrows. Now drink in this teaching and feel your unity with the words and the world of a guru.

Everyone is worthy of God's grace. Do not deny yourself this gift, which is given unconditionally. The entire universe is in you, and though it is composed of various parts, it is all there for you to love and to become. It is all connected. If you hurt your little finger, your whole body hurts. If you hurt another living being, you hurt yourself. If your heart hurts, your guru's heart hurts. We are all one in the same reality.

Right now you experience a small part of God in your life, whether you know it or not. Why not enter into God's love and experience the whole of it? The part or the whole, which will it be? As I said at the beginning, you can only run after the parts for so long before you understand that only the whole will satisfy you. As you come closer and closer to knowing the whole, the wonder of it all keeps you in constant awe and God-bliss. In God's abundance, every moment is fresh and new.

To look for satisfaction outside of yourself is to strive. To be calm in the arms of the Mother is one of the highest achievements in life. For every problem there is an answer that has its roots in God. Every religion teaches this. No questions can come about without the answer already being there, in *you*. You need only to be calm and listen to the voice within. Learning to be calm and aware, no matter what life places before you, prepares you to be calm and aware even in death.

To be aware of the power of your consciousness is a great achievement which you can work toward, beginning now. When you find yourself running after glory and money and the many other inviting things of the world, stop for a moment and be grateful for all you have. By becoming aware of all the blessings in your life, you can change your destiny. Your life can change this very moment if you are positive instead of always complaining.

It is a great thing to be able to relate to your own God-consciousness at any given moment, and this is a miracle that can be yours. Cleanse your heart of any negativity and make ready for the Mother to come and dwell there. God created you to be with her all of your life and into death and into life again and again, if you so choose. Coming back is a matter of the karma that you yourself create. You are the maker of your own destiny; you are the maker of who you think you are.

Never become one of those people who can never be wrong. Admit to your mistakes and learn how not to make them again. This is the wise way to live. This is the way to live in God. You can be the holiest of the holy if you just keep your heart open. God will bring to you a love that is beyond anything of this earth if you fill yourself every day with compassion for all beings of this world.

In you there is the magnificent creative force of the Mother's shakti. The moment you understand that you are the Mother's child, you will be able to see your own beauty. I can tell you this, but the guru's job is not to teach you. It is to remind you of what you already know, and everything you need to know is deep within you.

Expanding Who You Are

If you sit very quietly in the early dawn, you can hear the Mother beckoning. Listen to her call you and resolve to meet yourself, your real Self, without any more delay.

The second you can feel that you are an extension of God the Mother and God the Father, your life expands. To know how close you are to God liberates you from fear, and when you are freed from fear, sorrow cannot touch you as deeply as it once did. Instead, you will whisper the name of God to your heart throughout the day.

Do you feel that *maya* (illusion) has trapped you in your body? Do you feel limited by your body and mind? And do you feel this maya trying to hold on? Do not be afraid of maya. You can tell the difference between reality and illusion by listening to your heart. You can go beyond your body and mind and venture into your true being by becoming firmly established in the love that God has given you to live life fully.

The yogi is one who is awake in self-awareness. The yogi is one who chooses to be awake.

Spirituality has to be felt in every part of your being, not as something just taught to you but as something you experience. As you get to know God's great light, you also get to understand yourself in a new and wonderful way. You can be on the path for many, many years and lifetimes, and all of a sudden it hits you: I am not this body, yet I am this body and so much more. With this new yet ancient understanding, you begin a deeper journey on the same path. You make a commitment to hear yourself from the depth of your soul.

Standing in this consciousness of the Mother, and filled with dignity and divinity, you begin to recognize who you are, and you want to spread the strength and joy of this knowledge to others.

But first, you have to want to give up your suffering. You have to want to give up your grief. You have to want to give up your guilt. It does not matter what you have done in your life as long as you learn deeply from your mistakes. You need only make a commitment to yourself that you will not make the same mistakes over and over.

You have to want to be happy and joyful, and more than anything else you have to want to share God's bliss.

Happiness in God is never insecure. Depend on it, and be productive. Be in harmony and know that your life is rich. Let the joy in your life allow you to share with another who needs this happiness. A moment of sharing will enrich your life as well.

Walking the spiritual path of kindness, do not be afraid to let your heart open more and more. One way to open the heart is to learn to hesitate before saying words that will bring grief to others. You will find then that your words will comfort rather than hurt. Never hide your words of compassion; always express them, because the shakti of words comes from the Mother, from the Self within that always has been.

Judge no one, not even yourself. Remember that love sees only God in everyone, and God sees only love in you. Realize who you are—an extension of God. Realize that you have been given a body in order to work through karma. You have been given another chance to get things right. If you can learn from your mistakes, then faith will hold a deeper place in your life.

Never let yesterday interfere with today. Faith in yourself has nothing to do with the past, because the faith I speak of is alive and well in the present moment, and this moment is so big.

As you make your way along the spiritual path, much is unveiling itself. Without the pressure of the ego and all its subtle desires, the mind uncovers its own great want, the thirst for God. As you experience moments that are free of ego, even though they are just moments, know that they are signs of how far you have come. When you are free of ego, you are humble, and to be humble is a high state of being, because it allows you to move ever closer toward God.

How many times have you kept yourself away from God? How many times have you allowed yourself to be swept up by the problems in your life and forgotten to be calm? Give this up immediately. The small ego that clings to its problems has to be put in balance with God's love; then it becomes the higher Self and has the wisdom to let go. There is so much happiness in your heart if only you are aware. Then once aware, you will bring God-happiness to others just by being alive. Be always aware of your higher Self and live in peace.

INTERLUDE

Shiva Ratri

SHIVA RATRI

Outdoors by the sacred fire, we celebrate Shiva Ratri, the holy night of the great Lord Shiva, whose dance on one foot creates and spins out the swirling universe; the great Lord Shiva, god of the yogis, who sits absorbed in meditation atop Mount Kailash, his ash-besmeared body as white as the surrounding snow, as white as the light streaming from the crescent moon that adorns his brow. Shiva Ratri—a night of forgiving, a night of loving, a night of becoming one with God.

Shiva reigns as king, the great king of Kashi. Lord Shiva is higher than death and greater than life. Are we not all children graced by the Lord? Who is your Lord? Is it Jehovah? Is it Allah? Is it Shiva? Or is it the formless God that we all want so deeply that our very bones ache for the flesh of God's name? Taste the essence of a still night like this. God is to be enjoyed. Ritual is to be loved. And yet, it is always the moment that brings the most fulfillment.

In this unadorned moment of loving God in gratitude for our lives, we dive into our truth, our prayers, and our worship. The moment swells, pregnant with ecstasy. Let every one of you be touched by your God. Whoever you are, gather the blessings. Whomever you believe in, acknowledge your God in the sacred space between your eyebrows. If that God has no form, then feel the very essence of nature, of love, of the fulfillment of loving God, of loving the Goddess.

I look around at our Kashi shrines: at the Christ with his arms embracing us all; at our Jewish temple, with her arms embracing us all; at Mother Kali; at Lord Hanuman; and at the Shiva lingam, symbol of the ultimate light. And I acknowledge our Neem Karoli Baba, my guru.

May you all be blessed on this Shiva Ratri, this holy night. For this is not the night only of Lord Shiva, but also of Shakti, his consort, who said to him, "I am your wife. Emerge from your meditation and acknowledge me, for I am all movement, I am all truth, I am all trust. Acknowledging me, you will indeed acknowledge the world."

On this night let us be blessed, but more than that, let us feel the blessing.

Behold the flame of the sacred fire. Look at the great beauty of it. The beauty is that we control it, we control it with our worship and with our prayers. This night, throw into that flame everything by which you judge yourself.

And now I turn to the *linga*, Lord Shiva's great symbol, and say, "Touch me. Touch me with your grace and your profound beauty." The shaft of light goes into you. May you never be without it. May you never forget that you are Shiva and also Shakti. You are the perfect union of the masculine and feminine. Accept yourselves as you are.

The vast, open book of acceptance is so much greater than the book of ignorance. It contains the fullness of embracing all paths, all ways, all colors, all creeds, all religions, all sexuality. In it we find the wisdom to ease our wounded, torn hearts.

I am the Mother of thousands of gay and lesbian children and everything in between. To me, that is the true interfaith path—that I can say those words, that I can be those words, that I will live those words as I have always done. I make a home for all people who wish to learn of acceptance and the joy of loving God. And I will grow myself as I learn more and more about everyone else's path.

Who is this God who bears witness to us all, who knows our heart?

No name. Just a moment.

Who is this God who judges no one, condemns no one, but accepts all? No name. Just a moment.

Who is this God who hears you?

No name. Just a moment.

Who is this Goddess whose breasts are filled with milk, who weeps when you cry, laughs when you have joy?

No name. Just the moment.

Is this God called the moment? No moment. Just stillness.

Is this Goddess called stillness? No stillness. Just.

Is she a just god? She is all gods.

Is he a righteous god? He is all gods.

What is scripture? All scriptures.

What is her path? All paths.

I look around me and you are beautiful. How dare you condemn yourself by that which has been decreed in the past?

How dare you take no heed of this moment? Do you think you are too impure to receive the blessings of God?

God is magnificent. I don't know the God that judges. I don't know the God that condemns. I don't know the God that brings wrath down upon his own children. I only know the God of acceptance, the God of love. And I know that you are that which God has made you. Over and over I speak this truth.

I speak also the truth of the skull. The skull has no flesh. It has no eyes, yet it can see. It has no nose, yet it picks up all scents. The skull is my death, the death of the ego, death to the world. The skull is that which is finished, finished, finished. I am finished. I have become one with God, one with the formless. I have become One, period. There is no duality, no flesh on the bone.

PART TWO
Obstacles

Negativity

There are many different miseries in this world. There are some that you can do nothing about and some that you can do a great deal about. It depends on how generous you want to be with your time, your prayers, and yourself.

Without love we live with negativity, and so I ask you not to put into your heart anything that is filled with negativity and ingratitude.

The heart is your center of awareness. When the heart is filled with darkness and revenge, you can actually feel how shriveled it becomes. Such a heart is a breeding ground for hate and bigotry. Then the mind becomes crippled with anger, and what is the result? Only that you find yourself all alone in life.

When you live with thoughts of anger and revenge, you relive over and over the abuse or injustice that was done to you. You never get away from it. You never get rid of it. You are never at peace. Hate can never rid you of hate. If it leads you to inflict pain on others, then you inflict further pain on yourself.

The first thing to do is to recognize negativity the second it comes to you. You can get in the habit of catching negative thoughts by recognizing the oncoming sadness that usually comes with them. If your thoughts are filled with confusion, sit and simply say the name of your God or your guru or your spiritual guide, over and over until you are calm and clear.

When you can recognize that which is false, you can follow that which is true. As soon as negativity comes bursting in, you can consciously change your thoughts and become the master of your own nature. Why linger in negativity? Why settle for lesser things when you can look for the depth in your own being?

Sometimes a negative thought will arise from past karma. You need to get to know your own heart and to become familiar with your God-given soul. Developing a positive attitude every day of your life, you begin to discover the natural insight you were born with. You begin to find a wonderful quality within yourself and to have joy in it. God in the form of the Divine Mother is the supreme quality, and her presence within you drowns out all negativity.

With insight into your personality, you will be able to change that which you do not need. For a full and spiritual life, when you sit in meditation, convert all negativity into thoughts of love. Breathe deeply into your heart and think of the way you love life, God, guru, teacher, or anything else that will lighten your mood.

Let the breath help you to become aware. The breath does not hold negativity for very long. The breath that comes from deep within can only carry thoughts of goodness and love.

As you listen and grow, the root of sorrow can be destroyed. Past karmas lose their power in the light of spiritual awareness. Positive thoughts can wash away negative thoughts and prevent negative actions. As you think gratefully about positive things, negative sentiments such as anger, greed, jealousy, and pride begin to fade away. The mind will reject thoughts of violence or greed or jealousy.

When your tension is greater than your relaxation, stress takes hold of you, and you come apart quickly. You can lose focus, judgment, and self-control. But when you focus on your breath, you become more and more relaxed. You find intuitive wisdom in the midst of your chaos. Breathe again and again with awareness and joy. Take hold of the feet of the guru and know that you will never be alone again.

You are endowed with immense mental strength. When the mind tells you what it wants to do, be aware and never let its thoughts of fear or doubt rule you. Never let your own dark thoughts cripple you. When you allow negative thoughts into your life, you only narrow the scope of your existence. There is no reason ever to let this happen.

First feed the mind with positive thoughts to break the cycle of negativity. Then focus on the breath and the heart, and let your heart tell you what you need to do.

As you learn by this practice to live in the moment, there is less and less that can agitate the mind. As you learn how to work with your negative emotions, they slowly disappear. It is time to free your mind from the inner turmoil that has followed you from lifetime to lifetime. Yet, do not expect this to happen all at once. It happens slowly and beautifully.

Keep busy when negativity threatens to come on you. Remind yourself each day, "I will have patience, I will have patience." If you do this for only a few moments at a time, these words can change your life. First be kind and patient with yourself, and then you will certainly be kind and patient with others. If you like, pray to Tara, the Mother of Compassion, to bring you to the place of your heart where you will always have compassion for yourself and for others.

As you begin to unravel your problems, your life changes. Inner conflict becomes a thing of the past, and inner peace takes its place. You get a feeling for your essential nature of love and truth, and you develop the ability to manifest that deepest part of you. You bring to the surface of your life the very soul of who you are. When you are in charge of yourself, your genuine creativity, which you have kept hidden for so many years, is ready to emerge. You can create a beautiful universe.

You have within you the ability to teach yourself the true value of life. Remember this day your positive experiences even if they seem so very small, like finding a flower or a leaf with beautiful color. When you think of positive experiences, the negative ones are overshadowed, then crowded out. You may not see the process happening, yet all at once you know that you have rid yourself of something that you did not need at all and that you clung to only because you were afraid of change.

If you live in your heart the way your guru has taught you, then change can become a beautiful experience.

Negativity is only an illusion. Remember always that the spirit within your being is free from all defects. Celebrate your freedom from anger, stress, and negativity. Know that your spirit is perfect and you need only to tap into it to find harmony within yourself. Then there is nothing that you cannot overcome.

The Undisciplined Mind

Whatever we look at, we look at with our mind. If you begin to change that and look at things with your heart instead, then your life slowly begins to change for the better. There is a reason for this: thought from the mind divides things and brings duality, but thought from the heart brings all together as the One.

If you let your mind run free, it will become your master. That is because the mind would much rather be involved with the illusion of maya than merge into the oneness of God.

The senses keep the mind involved with the world, but the mind can be stilled by controlling the senses through awareness of the breath. Get into the habit of following the breath in and out, and think of it as the tender touch of God.

To control the senses through the breath is to still the mind, and to still the worldly mind is to experience the universal mind, to feel the reality of the Self.

Meditation should be simple, but what do you do? Do you not actually design your own thoughts so you won't have to sit for long periods of time? You sabotage yourself every time you let your ego step in to keep you from knowing your true Self.

The ego really does not know much, but it is clever and it knows what will hurt you and keep you away from God. What can we do? We find an answer in the work of the poet Ram Prasad: "This time I shall devour thee utterly, Kali Ma." By devouring the Mother, you devour the world; by devouring the world, you devour your own thoughts; and then you can drink in the nectar of your own beauty.

You have spent your life relating to your mind. Begin relating instead to the Self. There is great freedom in allowing its power, its shakti, to run free in your being. This Shakti is none other than the Divine Mother. Breathe into your heart and bring in the essence of shakti. Ask the Mother in any of her many forms to grant you *ananda*, a state of being where you are constantly in the bliss of God. Relax the mind, relax the body, and let the breath out all the way. Do this for seven full breaths and feel the joy.

Be clear this moment and see how much easier it is to be in the heart than in the mind. One moment in the heart dismantles all negativity, because everything that brings agitation to your being is based on thought.

In the world you must make decisions, but if you remember to breathe into the heart first, you send away all negative thoughts. You recognize that it is not the mind that leads you along the spiritual path but the heart.

Thought has no power over love, and everything that brings love to you and everyone else arises from the heart.

Remember always that you are a part of infinity. Never limit yourself, but expand, expand, expand and feel free on your sacred path.

What Are You Thinking?

Your own thinking can take you along your spiritual path, or it can take you from your path.

First you think, and then you put your thought into action. By allowing the same old wrong thoughts to be put into action over and over again, you continue to make the same basic mistake. That mistake is forgetting that you, and not your circumstances, are supposed to be dictating your life.

In everyone there is a space unknown to the ordinary consciousness of worldly life, unknown until the spiritual teacher decides to introduce the student to the greatness it holds. The teacher lights a flame within the spiritual seeker. This flame will lead you whenever you are in need. A symbol or reality? Neither and both. It depends on when you are ready to hear that the whole of the universe is within you, and that you are the whole universe.

Then it happens. The lower mind comes in, saying, "I am not smart enough. I am not rich enough. I am not pretty enough. I am not handsome enough. I am not worthy." This is a trick of the ego-mind when you ignore the heart. The ego-mind creates all sorts of obstacles on your path to God—obstacles like anger, greed, delusion, conceit, jealousy, and desires of a lower nature. Trap those thoughts and offer them to the Mother. Bring your attention back to the flame and follow it back to the space in the heart.

Whenever you feel inspired to return to the quiet of this hidden space, know that you are open to receiving its inspiration. You begin living a bigger life. After a while the space comes to you, and you find that you are surrounded by the luxury of knowing. Yes, the knowing comes to you in all its abundance and unfolds in a way that is nothing short of a miracle.

When this hidden space, unknown for so long, is yours to command, then there is no darkness—only light. There is no judgment—only the moment.

Those who glory in self-centeredness deceive themselves. Right thinking can confront all self-deceptions. In this practice a good thought, such as a thought of love, will take root and become a "not-thought" and a spontaneous action. Once you get into the habit of right thinking, it is easier to give up thoughts altogether. At first, dark thoughts may come into view when you least expect them, but only for a while.

There is a sacred energy that runs through you like India's holy River Ganga and nourishes your thinking. Could this be called God-thinking? When a thought such as "God loves me and everything about me" is planted in the holy soil of the heart, it takes root and ends all feeling of separation. Ask yourself how any type of separation can produce harmony between you and the world or between you and God.

All thoughts other than God-thoughts are merely a habit which promotes more habits that lead to negative actions. Such thoughts can fall apart by thinking of the sacred Ganga, for they get drenched in the Mother's holy waters. If you don't understand these words, just consume them with your heart and let your God-mind make them clear.

Thought is only one element of your existence, but it is very powerful. It can turn your life into one of trust or one of fear. Fear is the direct result of thinking fearful thoughts. Whenever you have negative thoughts, you put time and effort into them and make them into a reality. Your reality becomes negative, and negativity rules your life.

I remember when my Baba first told me always to approach the guru and feel the guru's love before allowing myself to feel any negative thoughts. In this way you can turn all thoughts into positive ones. When you put time and effort into positive thoughts, you make them into a reality. You are the maker of your own thinking and the maker of your own destiny. What you think is what you become.

Understanding this, you can conquer anything and everything. Your ability to overcome all circumstances is deep inside you. Put your trust in the teachings you have received and call upon your teacher to help you dismiss negative thoughts. Then you can find the happiness you have always sought.

Anger—Yours and Others'

One of the signs of a worldly nature is anger. If you feel anger, ask yourself, are you really angry? Or are you just tired? Or are you just not in the moment?

Take the time to study your life and see if there are places within where you hold on to anger. You will find that these places have a hold on you. When angry feelings bubble up, just pause, and before you act, ask yourself, "Is this what I want to say? Is this what I want to do?" Then take a deep breath into your heart and feel how much you are loved by God and guru. Breathe in the light of love and get rid of the darkness.

When you become angry and allow outer things to come before your love of God, it is too easy to forget your great inner capacity to love yourself and others. Anger steals away joy, but the love of God sustains you in joy.

When you find anger welling up in you, take a deep breath and consider that for a few seconds your mind became irrational. An irrational mind can bring harm to you, your practice, and your life. Anger increases the dark energy of inertia, called *tamas*, so you cannot be creative when the mind is lost in anger.

The breath can open the heart and soothe the mind. If someone comes at you with deep anger, that can be a sign of dissatisfaction with life. Remember that most angers are toward one's self, and most likely the other person is just taking it out on you. And yet, never interpret someone else's anger. That kind of judgment usually makes matters worse.

When someone comes at you with negativity and anger, it is your choice not to react in the same way. It is your chance to dive into the Mother's light while the darkness of anger and vindictiveness approaches. Know that those who are cruel to others really are cruel to themselves. They are always in pain but do not understand that malice is its own punishment. If you make space for the anger to wane, you create the possibility for a moment of peace. On the other hand, if you react to another's anger, it will only grow and you will be drawn in, ensnared by it, and separated from your own peace. Remember always that anger wastes time and energy.

The most wonderful thing that you can do for your spiritual life is to free yourself from reactions. Do not react this day to anyone's anger, beginning with your own. Instead of reacting, take a moment to breathe in all the love in the world. Then breathe out all the love in the world. Look at how you can live fully and let all anger go.

Trust in this process, and know that such faith is of the moment. It does not matter what your past was; you can grab hold of faith now and reverse all karmas, all the results of your past deeds and your present habits. This trust is what gives you strength.

As you learn to become increasingly still in the moment, you change the quality of your life with the quiet of your being. You expand into a place without borders or judgments. When you speak, you speak from your heart. You become kind to everyone and take advantage of no one.

Still, as you go deeper and deeper into meditation, you may find internal irritation. This is a sign that you are bringing to the surface those things that you do not need. Often this happens so you can recognize that which keeps you from God. When you begin to understand that such matters are not important enough to become angry or annoyed about, they will not irritate you any more. When you can conquer one irritation, others will not be able to take root.

Is there something in you that sneaks up and destroys your moment? Is there something that you do over and over that can bring you into instant depression?

Now focus on your breath, and at the same time see something about yourself that you do not like. Breathe it out of the top of your head, and deliberately leave it out as you breathe in again.

Now ride the breath back to yourself, leaving behind what you do not need. From this simple exercise you can keep a certain vitality flowing all the time. Anger can drain your vitality, but if you place your anger on the breath and breathe it out, you can train yourself to be independent of anger and pain.

If you do not have anger, you cannot have hatred. Never forget that the true purpose of life is love. Bring that love to all people. Ask the Mother to keep your heart so open that anger will have no place in your life. Ask her to show you how to ask her for everything you need to succeed in your spiritual life and all of your life upon this wonderful Earth. Ask her to show you how to pray for peace for everyone in the world. Ask the Mother to show you how to attain communion with the universal divine Self.

Sometimes in the face of darkness you cannot see the goodness in others, but as long as you try to see goodness, then goodness will come to you. You can never become insensitive to the goodness of others, because love always leaves a powerful imprint on a person's heart. You can leave this imprint on the heart of others.

Light is love. In the end, it is light that always wins. Treasure your own ability to love everyone, and exert your best efforts when you deal with someone else's anger. Your heart has a deep well of wisdom that knows what to do. You need only hesitate before you react and feel the fullness of your own inner wisdom. Truly, you have more patience than you can even begin to understand. There is no reason for you to get caught in the net of anger. Instead, feel the freedom from anger that love can bring.

The simple fact is that love can melt all anger. Hold in your heart the oneness of love and remember that love is limitless. That is the amazing thing about love: the more of it you give away, the more you have.

Who Do You Think You Are?

The ego is the main troublemaker in worldly life and a major obstacle for the spiritual seeker as well.

What is the ego? It's who you think you are and everything that goes along with that. The ego, if you allow it, has the power to manipulate your emotions and make you feel overwhelmed with your life.

All the senses, through which you interact with the world, can be made negative by the ego. The action of the lower ego on the senses is that of a dark force seeping into a lighter one, for there is no negativity in the senses themselves. They just are, but their nature is to pull you outward into the world, where the involvement of your ego creates problems. When you let your ego fall into desire and allow the senses to rule you, it becomes very difficult to master them.

To begin, tell yourself that darkness has no place in your life. Yet all your experiences are darkened and made negative by the lower ego.

When you say, "I am this and I am that," you are speaking from your ego and not from your heart of awareness.

When you become possessive, that is the ego's possessiveness. When you try to possess others or make them accept your truth as their truth, you only bind yourself. When you do not try to possess others or make them accept your truth as their truth, then you become ever more free.

The ego and a healthy sense of self are not the same thing. When your thoughts keep going back to a past hurt or insult over and over again, everything begins to stick to your mind. You get lost in the possessiveness of all your negative thoughts, and then you begin to react to others with anger.

Let the heavy stones of their judgment of you fall away. Why should you ever have let them burden you in the first place? Do not hold on to the opinions of others that can quickly devour your own good feelings. Remember that your spiritual worth has nothing to do with what others think of you. *Do not react, either with your body or your mind.*

When you are struggling to give up your own negativity, do not judge others. Never become bitter toward others, and be very aware of hate. Otherwise you will just welcome all the darkness back into your life and litter your path to liberation with many obstacles.

Instead, look at your heart and feel the love there. It is your greatest gift. Nothing can hurt you when you are aware of the Mother's love. God will love you no matter what; embrace her love. Discover your true self-worth apart from the lower ego, and know that you are perfect as you are this day. If you let her, the Mother will teach you to turn your anger to love, your greed to giving, your delusion to truth, your conceit to humility, your jealousy to sharing, and all your desires of a lower nature to the pure desire for holiness. When you take the time to listen to the Mother's voice of wisdom within your own heart, then she will teach you that the attachment of ego brings terrible pain. When you are not so attached, your pain will lessen and lessen.

The ego's voice is the voice of deception. It leaves no space for peace of mind or soul. Attachment to objects brings fear of their loss. Attachment to being right all the time creates distress in you and discomfort in others. Therefore, stagger out of this wilderness of the ego's wants and enter into Mother Kali's sacred cremation ground. There let the ego and all its desires burn to ash and blow away with the wind of the Mother's grace. All that you do not need will vanish into her unblemished sky of consciousness.

The Mother Kali is an awesome force of love, and you will never be unfulfilled if you heed her voice within your heart. Do not let the ego deceive you into thinking that you are not worthy of God's love. Instead, let the ego die on Mother Kali's funeral pyre.

However old you are or however young, you can change your life for the better right now. You only have to love yourself enough to be open to the love that is offered to you. You have to love yourself enough to be willing to give up what you do not need. Does the lower ego make you cling to negativity or feelings of unworthiness? If you do not appreciate your own life and feel thankful for it, you have nothing to give to the world.

Great lives are not created by the ego. Great lives are not necessarily those of the powerful or the famous. Great lives become great from the heart and soul. Everyone has the ability to live a great and wonderful life.

"How do I do this?" you ask.

First, you make space in your day to meditate. Be stimulated by meditation and spirituality. You will feel changes in yourself almost immediately. Meditate on your wholeness. I say "wholeness," because when you leave all the illusions of ego behind, you become connected to the infinity of the Divine Mother. You leave behind your illusions of smallness and isolation and imperfection. You release the self-destructive tendencies that are of the ego, not of your true Self. I, your Ma, can see beauty in every one of you. Dig deep and find your own great beauty.

Until you have reached deep into the heart of your being and found the inner light of the Self, you remain a bound soul, seeking bliss. Because of the ego you are ignorant of who you truly are. Where there is ignorance, there is bondage. It's as simple as that.

Put your breath in harmony by practicing deep breathing, and you will begin to control the ego-based impulses. As the purity of this teaching reaches through you and embraces your body, mind, and soul, you can feel the Mother's grace taking hold of your heart. In any form you know and love, the Mother is present. She is in your heart and in everything you see. Never separate your thoughts about you from thoughts about God the Mother.

If you feel separate, you are not yet seeing the great love you hold in your heart. As you breathe in and out of your heart, know that *you* are the love.

Feel the connection to God. *You* are the connection.

Feel the stillness. *You* are the stillness.

When you are purified of ego, you will recognize that you are the universal Self. You will know supreme joy. You will know that you are unborn, undying, and all-pervading.

Now breathe in the joy of the egoless state, and from then on let God the Mother do her work through you.

Take refuge in the supreme Self. It is always just a breath away. Just as waves cannot hide the ocean, all the circumstances of your life cannot hide the Self.

As you meditate on the Self, the Self will become more and more familiar—familiar because it is your true being. You are the beauty of the Self. Allow this day and every day to unfold the wondrous qualities of your being.

Ingratitude

When I see that something stands in the way of a person's happiness, most often what I see is ingratitude. Ingratitude is one of the greatest obstacles on the path to God. It limits one's life, and its particular kind of limitation stunts and cripples. Ingratitude brings on a deep, self-destructive anger as you forget to feel love toward those who love you. After a while disrespect for others seeps in and darkens your mind. This is a terrible burden to carry around.

When you forget that someone has helped you in any way, or when you cast judgment on others who have always been there for you, your heart will never be filled. Never allow yourself to be limited in this way. The mind that resents and judges brings separation. Where there is separation, love cannot flow.

43

Whenever you seek instant gratification for your own selfishness, then also you begin to feel separated from those who love you and from God also. This is when you really need to approach the holy moment of the breath and make your acquaintance with your inner being. As you become aware of your breath, listen to your own God-voice. The two are connected. You can never undo this connection, yet you must have the willingness to be consistent in your mindfulness. This practice increases love in your heart and awareness in your life.

Living in God brings an end to the separation that causes pain, and the closer you get to your own heart, the closer you are to the destruction of the shell of separation that is the ego-self. It will melt away in the heat of devotion, and love will lead you to the non-duality of the Self.

The God who is kind and gracious is that same graciousness within your own Self. Once you find the real you, you bring your life into that space of divine graciousness, and then you end your own sense of isolation. When the obstacles are removed from the path to God, you become free in your giving of love and affection. You will never again let your heart harden. You will never again shut yourself off from others. You will never again take advantage of anything or anyone. The heart that is grateful is the heart that keeps remembering love. Such a heart is gentle, open, and full.

God acknowledges your love in so many different ways. One of the many ways you can acknowledge God's love is to be aware. One way that brings you to this awareness is gratitude. Gratitude swiftly brings the thought of God to the heart, in a flash. Be grateful to God for all you have in your life. No matter how full your mind is of things to be done, the heart can always make room for a moment of gratitude. If you are feeling troubled, it is so important to remember that the one thing that can stop the flow of the Mother's compassion is ingratitude.

Remember that nothing is impossible through God's love. That love is free of judgment and free of conditions.

My guru Neem Karoli Baba is the essence of unconditional love and compassion. He teaches us to serve in the name of God and to take care of all God's children. How? It is so simple. When you are compassionate, a special type of creativity enters your life. You naturally find ways to serve others, and when you can meet another's needs, then you are helping to create a better and more beautiful world. Even then, never be so preoccupied that you forget to thank God, for in this way you can keep your heart open all day long.

This day and every day have great appreciation for God and all of creation. Constantly be grateful for the small things you have taken for granted until now. Find God everywhere and in everyone. Know that you are connected to all things of earth and heaven and that there are no limits in your life. Make this day like no other.

Think of how wonderful it is to have a human life, and show your gratitude by serving someone with all the love in your heart. Throughout the day do your work with joyous detachment, and whenever you get a chance, turn your mind inward and think on the Mother Kali. Feeling drenched in her love, reflect on the beauty in your life. Seek holy company, and you will be sure to taste the joy of community. Sing to the Divine Mother and hear her sweet voice reply in your heart. At the end of the day, when you lay your head down to sleep, remember to thank God the Mother and God the Father for everything and everyone in your life.

Therefore, hold the light of gratitude in every cell of your being. Can you ever be too grateful? Never! When thankfulness becomes your way of being, it lifts you to a new level of spiritual wholeness and continual newness in your life. As gratitude purifies the mind and opens the heart to new possibilities of love and service and awareness, it is the key to all paths to God.

Things Aren't as They Seem

The world consists of layers of illusion, maya, that only the full heart can cut through.

The unenlightened mind creates many an illusion, and these waves of deception will keep you in pain and anger. Life is hard when you identify with unreality, yet that is what most people do most of the time. Through the veils of illusion you see what you want to see and think what you want to think. You think about all those things that you want to possess, and you believe that having those things will make you happy and whole. Yet in the end, this illusion can only bring you pain, because it will fail to satisfy you for very long. Illusion is like a shell of separation that surrounds you and keeps you from breaking through to what you really want—the wholeness that comes from loving God.

The Mother Kali wields a sharp sword, called the sword of knowledge. This sword is your own love of God that cuts away all that you do not need. The first step to be taken on your path is to recognize what makes you unhappy and to see through the impermanence of that thought. Attachment is illusion. The Mother's sword of knowledge will help you to cut through that illusion and gain freedom from clinging to all that is impermanent. Do not cling to thoughts of doubt or fear or anger or shame; do not let them regulate your existence. Instead, feel the miraculous daily, and never separate yourself from God. Acknowledge your own beauty, and make the basic changes in your life that you long for, knowing that you have the freedom to do so.

No matter what you may think, you have no real relationship with illusion. The true relationship of your heart is with the God and Goddess within your being. An important step into the reality of the heart is seeing the false as false. What does that mean? It means asking yourself who you are.

What will you find in the reality of the heart? There you will discover your own beauty, your own inner spirit. It is the illusion of ego that will not allow you to recognize your own greatness, just as much as it is the illusion of ego that blows your idea of yourself up out of all proportion. Either way, the illusion is ignorance of who you truly are.

To sum up, by ignoring your own inner spirit you bring conflict and unhappiness into your life. Do not be bound by the limitations of time and space but reach beyond them. If you expect to find happiness in your possessions or in your attachments to other people, I will tell you this: never look to find permanence in your possessions; never look to find permanence in your attachments to other people. Permanence is only in God. Everything else is subject to change, and no one can put a stop to change. To seek permanence in the things of life is to waste time by chasing after illusions. You will never quench your thirst by running after a mirage.

Instead, seek serenity even in the midst of chaos or confusion. You can do this by bringing your focus to the functioning of your inner life. Through *bhakti*, your heart's devotion, you can turn your attention to communicating with God the Mother and God the Father. You can convert the ever-changing moments of time into the moment of God's permanence beyond all illusion.

Karma

Did you know that you have a great treasure chest within your being? This treasure chest is filled with your own memories of past lifetimes. These impressions are the reality of all your lifetimes, and they hold deep insight into all your past attachments.

Negative thoughts bury themselves deep in the subconscious and rise up when you least expect them to. They surface as all kinds of feelings, and when you meditate, they emerge ever more clearly. Yet there is always the grace of God, guru and *paramaguru* (the guru's guru), and the grace of your own mind. When you sit in meditation, you can burn out the negativity with the great light of God. Negativity is easy to get rid of if you know in your heart that you are loved by God.

With the regular practice of meditation and *pranayama* (controlled breathing), there is nothing you cannot accomplish.

You have been the great author of your past lives, yet you are also the author of your present life and the life that will come to you in the future. The great secret of karma is to learn how to live and die surrendered to God at every moment. Everyone can be the architect of his or her moments through this simple act of surrendering the ego with all its will and judgment.

Each moment you live, whatever happens in life is absorbed in your unconscious and conscious mind. This includes the lessons you learn on the spiritual path. Everything you do has some sort of karma involved, and there are many kinds of karma. There are major karmas and minor karmas, but basically it is all about taking responsibility. The small realities of everyday living are just as important as the main events. You see, you are controlled by the karma that you create. Karma brings about the circumstances of your lives and also your reaction to those circumstances.

If something does not go well, do you react with anger? Through karma, whatever happens during your day is drawn to you, the person involved.

Never allow yourself to be stopped by negativity. If you fail to control your anger, do not despair, but let this failure become a lesson in life. Do not wait for time to solve your problems of anger, but offer them up now to the Mother Kali. Become fearless in your love for God, Goddess, and humanity, and you will see your anger devoured. Soon you will be able to control yourself and not react to the anger of others. When the mind becomes purified by your heart of love, the mind and heart become integrated. When the Mother takes your fear, she brings you courage in ways you would never believe. Then you can rise above any negative currents and surmount the lingering effects of all negative past actions.

Blend your meditation on love with the process of action, and serve humanity as your heart opens ever wider. Enlighten your heart also with the association of others who are on the spiritual path. As you have created your present through your past actions, you have the choice of the kind of future you will create for yourselves.

The Smallness of You

Sometimes you may feel small and without strength. Everyone does. Never forget that the Self is not limited by the world or the mind. The Self has no boundaries. It is beyond all darkness. It is perfect and pure light. The Self is all-encompassing. It sustains every moment, and if you become aware of this, you will never feel crushed and powerless again. You are the Self.

But how easy it is to forget! Your personality lives on the edge of the Self, in the dimness away from its light. That is why it is so important to get in touch with the Self and feel your whole being expand.

When you feel you are limited, you become limited. There is no need to feel this way. As my Baba Neem Karoli taught me, "You are part of that universal light, and that light is all of you; you have only to remember this and feel this light all the time."

When you forget that you are beloved of God, you become controlled by attachments, crippled by loneliness, and exhausted by the separation from the light. But when you feel that the breath can take you straight to the heart of God, then you cannot fail at anything you do.

Watch out especially for jealousy. Only you can arouse jealousy in your heart. When it flares up, it becomes much more than you intended it to be. You may have started it, but before long it controls you and then consumes you. Before it comes to this, see if you can find its roots.

When you are afflicted with jealousy, it is only because you are dissatisfied with yourself. Go deep into your heart, and you will see that you already have within you everything you need for happiness. There is no reason to be eaten up by jealousy. When you calm down your jealous mind and open your heart to love for those around you, you will find that jealousy is all an illusion, and the fullness of God is the reality. Let the illusion go, let your own sense of limitation go, and the reality will be yours in all its abundance.

Everyone gets older and eventually dies, yet the Self is always there and continues on and on, ever blissful, ever the same. Every person depends on lifetimes past to be in the present moment. It has been a long journey to this point. Yet if you are filled with the love and joy of God, you are creating in this very moment your future in God and Goddess. As you live ever closer to the loving heart of the Beloved, you begin to realize the great truth of the oneness of us all. You can become the source of compassion and love for all you meet, and you will begin to understand the greatness of the Self.

There is no victory more satisfying than the victory over the limits of the personality.

The heart can expand and expand to hold the universe. Inside of you is everything that is outside of you. What are your limitations? They are nothing but the shadows of your personality. When you lived on the edge of the Self, you dared not approach its brilliant light. Now you understand that the world you want to experience is the world that lives within you.

All positive actions add up and can never be in vain. Keep on with your life in God, and feel in your heart all the love that there is in the universe. The human heart wants desperately to abide in God, but the thoughts of the mind sometimes stand in the way. Expand the heart-awareness and know that the heart of God within you brings more abundant peace and love than you ever thought you could achieve on your own. What you must understand is that God loves to abide in you and to be recognized through all your actions. Enrich your life with the constant practice of selflessness.

To serve with a full and open heart in the name of God is to be in the divine presence. It is to be in God-consciousness, whatever form your idea of God may take. Compassion arises from this consciousness, and compassion is an open invitation to the goodness and bliss of God. Engage yourselves in serving others, and you will enlighten your mind and heart by easing their sufferings.

With the Mother's shakti you can accomplish anything in life. Look above you and know that the unlimited love in your heart is as vast as the blue, far-reaching sky. The Mother is always there and always here in the heart, and with her grace all the limitations you feel will melt away.

The Ticking Clock

When you have something to do and you keep putting it off, that is procrastination. Whenever you feel overwhelmed by the problems in life, just remember that once you get into the habit of putting them off until tomorrow, they become harder and harder to deal with, and your habit of procrastination becomes harder and harder to give up. Whatever you keep putting off becomes more and more painful, because you are never free of it.

When procrastination becomes a habit, your mind is habitually clouded with painful thoughts and your inner beauty begins to fade. When you fall prey to painful thoughts and put off doing something about them, you open up huge spaces for addictions. Procrastination is not in your genes. It is a habit that you created and one that you can break with sufficient awareness.

Keeping busy with that which is important is one way to make your life worthwhile.

Procrastination means saying "not now" to that which needs to be done. You all know what you need to do, so just do it. Always make time for your spiritual practice. Otherwise, procrastination will have you waking up one day and finding out that you have wasted your life.

Live the teachings you have been given, *now!* Try to do all things as they come before you, and you will be surprised at how satisfying this can be. It will help to break the old habit of putting things off and create a new habit of mindfulness. When you become successful in your spiritual practice, you can know for certain that you did not procrastinate. You did not waste your time and energy on a host of bad habits.

The source of awareness is in you, and you start to be aware through watching your breath. I cannot say this enough: *the breath, the breath, the breath.* Ride the breath back to your inner awareness. Once you understand that happiness is already in you and you only need to stir it up, then you will not let negativity occupy any space within your being. This will bring you to the moment.

How do you live in the moment? By letting the past go. By not worrying about the future. The past has passed, and the future has not happened. The now is all you have, and the now is awareness. Why wait? Why let procrastination steal this from you?

Stress and Anxiety

At times everyone feels stress. When you feel tight all over, it is hard for you to be in your heart; yet if you allow yourself to become bitter and negative, you will not even realize that your heart is closed.

Stress restricts the natural flow of God. Being in the Mother's simple moment brings you to wholeness and completion.

When your mind is out of the present moment, fear and want and stress may enter in. When you are out of the moment, you seek those things that you think will bring satisfaction. When you are in a state of anxiety, you are more likely to make the wrong choices. That is why all the circumstances of daily living are best dealt with without stress.

The heart of awareness inside you needs no education; it always knows what to do. Right choices seek no goals, for they do not look outside the moment.

When stress comes into your life, take a moment to see what is happening inside of you. Are you excited to start something new, or are you too tense?

Relax and breathe into the places in your body wherever there is discomfort. Roll your shoulders back four times, then roll them forward. Breathe in and out of your heart, and try to bring comfort to yourself this moment. Feel that you are being comforted by your spiritual teacher, and understand in the depth of your soul that you are loved.

Be detached from any troubling thoughts. Give them no time at all. They are not worth it. Acknowledge your love for your life, and let all sadness go.

Now bring your awareness to the spot between your eyebrows, and begin to feel a light there. Follow it as it travels downward into your heart. All the while, breathe deeply and easily. Now, with your attention centered in the heart, be friendly and loving to yourself. Remember that you are God's child, loved by God. Why shouldn't you love yourself?

Fear is at the root of much stress. Is there any fear in your heart? If so, breathe deeply into the belly and bring the breath up to your heart. Then breathe out from the heart. In this moment feel your whole body relaxed and free from stress.

Keeping the attention on the heart, breathe in deeply with awareness, breathe out deeply with awareness, and feel that your heart is stretching open. Breathe again into the heart and breathe out all the dark clouds of tension. Now you are experiencing joy— God-joy, God-love, God-happiness. When you breathe in again, feel you are breathing in only light and joy. You are free to send this same light and joy to anyone in the world.

The relaxation you seek is found between the breaths. This space of infinite quiet widens as you meditate more and more each day. Love breathes through this space between the breaths and takes you into the Mother's heart. Feeling this space in the present moment evokes more and more love in you, that same love that is the driving force of all truly holy people.

Living in the present moment, you realize the perfection already in everything. In the now you are never preoccupied or defeated, but wide open to the Mother's blessings, which make you whole and complete. Only the moment brings you everything.

When Life Hurts

When suffering comes, sometimes you think that you cannot get past that time of pain or grief. Yet if you take a moment to breathe into your heart, you will know that you can get past anything at all.

When suffering comes, sometimes you beg to have all the pain and grief disappear, but when you do this, you may be forgetting to honor your own inner strength. It is possible to give up pain and grief by not holding on to them. Such a simple truth is easy to overlook.

One of the reasons we feel our own pain so deeply is that we are unaware of the pain that others suffer. From the beginning of time people have been taught to reflect on their lives, and as we begin to understand our own pain, the heart opens wide and we can understand the pain of others. A deeper understanding of other people's grief keeps one's own heart full and flowing. With reflection on managing the anxiety and pain of others comes a deeper understanding of our own pain. How to make life easier for another being? It is all very simple. What would you want others to do for you?

As you serve, the pain in your heart is transcended and consumed as fuel. All of life is a continuous effort and a journey in which we learn to live better and do better for ourselves and others, and sometimes grief is the great teacher of how to live in love.

You can learn from suffering, but is it not better to learn from life before suffering happens? God's presence is evident if you just look around you with awareness and gratitude. You are the embodiment of eternal happiness; you only need to allow yourself to feel this. Bring yourself to God-consciousness by keeping the heart always open. Do this by opening your eyes to others and serving them, the Mother's children, in the name of the Mother.

If you do have suffering in your life, then know that you are strong enough to be in your heart, where the unconditional love of God and Goddess will bring you joy any time you seek it there. No matter what, God will never turn from you. That unconditional love is the grace of God in all her many forms. When you allow yourself to be open to it, and when you allow yourself to give it to others, you leave the prison of your own mind.

Live in the freedom and joy of God's love. This is the meaning of your life: to love every moment and to live your life from the inside out. Your life will constantly renew itself from inside of your being, and there will be no more room for pain and suffering.

Holding On Is Not Letting Go

Where there is attachment to the world, there is always fear and pain. The mind becomes agitated and can turn to anger. Any form of negativity is a form of attachment, and it is all too easy to become attached to negative habits. When you allow the mind to become attached, you give in to desires and cravings that can only hurt you.

If you let yourself become attached to the world, the world will make you sink into sorrow and grief. That is the confusion that comes with its illusion. If the senses are not controlled, spiritual expansion is very hard to acquire.

Never overlook the art of controlling the senses. It is not as hard as you may think. Keep the mind directed toward the divine presence within the heart, breathing quietly in and out, and feel your own inner calmness and peace. In this way you learn with great love, and not with striving, to control the senses.

There are two kinds of attachment: attachment to the world and attachment to God. The lower mind attaches itself to all things personal and of the world. The higher God-mind knows that attachment is possessiveness and not love. It knows that the freedom from detachment leads to liberation.

Ask in meditation, "Who am I?" Know that you are not this body, but the Self, always living, never dying. Know that you are the very strength that you search for, and become attached to the divine Self. This form of attachment is different from worldly attachment. This is your attachment to God, and attachment to God is no attachment at all. Remain always in your heart center, and allow your heart to shine with the great light of detachment.

Ask for nothing. No matter what happens to you, always maintain a grip on your heart and try to feel love. Whether life is bitter or sweet, practice maintaining a balanced mind in all conditions. This is turning to the insight that God the Mother has given to you. As you meditate on the freedom of detachment, wisdom is established in the heart. The greater the detachment, the closer you come to unconditional love and to the great experience of oneness.

Ask for nothing and feel everything. Detachment is not noncaring; in fact it is the opposite. To love another fully means not trying to possess and not even caring if you are loved in return. It means giving to others in the form of service. When you want nothing for yourself and everything for others, life becomes simple. You live in the simplicity of giving, taking, and serving always in the name of the Mother who lives deep in the heart. Your nonattachment will keep you always in a place of fullness and gratitude.

The Mother's radiant love, as unconditional as the sunlight, untangles all attachments born of ignorance. Freed from their complications, you have more time to love God devotedly, to take care of the poor and the hungry, and to remember that your essential nature is one with the Mother's goodness.

The Awful Need to Be Right

Are you attached to thoughts of always being right? The idea that you are attached to being right may not sit well with you. Yet I want you to look closely at your mind when you want so desperately to be right that you would sacrifice your own happiness. I have seen so many lives fall apart because someone wanted to be right.

When you pay attention to your negative thoughts, you begin to think that you are those thoughts. They take you into a place of pettiness, and you sink to the lowest level of thinking. Life stagnates in the shadow of negativity, and you become dismal. If you bottle up resentments or let anger become a permanent mark on your heart, do you know how dark and terrible that makes you look?

Do not insist on hanging on to your version of the truth. Never be a slave to circumstances that you yourself have created, but be ready to accept that someone else's ideas might be right. At least listen to them. It is a powerful practice to admit that you are not always right, to know that things can shift and change. If you find yourself getting angry or aggressive, remember that no one needs to be angry. No one needs to be aggressive. Why should you? Take a moment to breathe compassion for yourself into your heart and breathe out compassion for others.

Another practice is simply to let go of thoughts that cling like glue. If you say, "Mother Kali, take these thoughts from me," this will momentarily keep you out of the drama. If you can admit to yourself that perhaps you are wrong, there comes a freedom that allows you to inquire into the truth. Instead of being attached to your self-righteousness, let the Mother's love and wisdom dissolve the darkness of your confused mind, its endless running after "me" and "mine."

59

Recognize that thoughts are like passing clouds. Look up at the clouds in the great, clear sky, and take note of how the sky is not affected by them. Remember that you are like the sky, and remain detached and free. You are the vastness of the sky. Look at the sun, shining ever-brilliant even behind the clouds. Remember that you are like the sun, untouched by the passing clouds of life. You are the sun. Live every moment in the light of who you are. Let go of the need to be right and simply revel in the glory of you.

You can get rid of your dark ego-thoughts by giving them no heed. Pay no attention to them. Then even in times of anger or pain, such thoughts cannot remain for long but will be like the passing clouds. When they are gone, you remain in the stillness of the heart.

If you feel afraid, know that it is the ego that holds you back. Just sit like an inquisitive child and watch the thoughts come and go. When a thought that you do not like arises, say something opposite to it, and then watch the two thoughts disappear. Breathe love into your heart for a few breaths, then start all over. As the thoughts continue to flow in and out, say very gently, "Not now," and let them go like feathers in a gust of wind.

You can enjoy watching your mind, because that simple exercise can get rid of so much excess baggage. As you sit quietly and explore your mind, you will find growing insight and more compassion for yourself and others.

As you watch the breath coming in, going out, coming in, going out, and as your thoughts disperse, you will pass into simplicity. In the joy of simplicity you will no longer feel the need to be right.

The Outer World

Nonviolence begins with one person at a time. You must live in peace with yourself before you can live in peace with others. You must be willing to give up the dark energy that hurts you and those around you. You must be willing to let go of whatever obstructs you. Let the current of love flow freely from God to you, from you to God, from person to person. The very thought of not hurting others brings light to the darkest mind and brightens the moment.

If you allow thoughts of anger or violence to darken the mind, you work against your essential nature. When the mind is agitated by worldly concerns, you cannot access the calm depth of the heart.

Remember always that the mind should follow the heart; the heart should not follow the mind.

Whenever anxious or angry thoughts agitate you, say, "I am a child of the heart and the master of my mind." Repeat this until you feel that you are on top. Having calmed the mind, contemplate its anger, and ask if the angry mind brings you peace.

As you turn your mind to thoughts of peace, love and compassion will radiate from the depth of your soul and show you who you truly are. You are love, and love does not react with hate. You are peace, and peace brings peace to others. In the Mother's heart you live in the spirit of nonviolence and create a loving aura all around you.

The yoga tradition has a method of meditation that integrates the spiritual life with the life of the outer world. It is simple: God is never forgotten. The mantra, the name of God, is always in the heart. The words of the guru are always in the heart. It is hard to be angry when practicing this recollectedness. Be ever mindful that you are not your mind or your body or their worldly involvements.

Change your attitude this moment, and feel the lightness as the burdens fall away. Do not judge or blame others for what you do not like about you or your life. Your wealth and beauty are in your heart of awareness, for you to share with the world.

At this time the world needs love more than ever. Every heart must beat with the desire for peace. It is the responsibility of all of us every day to bring thoughts of peace to the world. Open your heart like never before, consciously direct your life-breath deep into the heart center, feel the heart expand, and let the breath out to the world, asking God to let your love be a healing force.

How wonderful it would be to see the sun rise each morning, knowing that it shines on peace all over the world. In that world there would be no hunger, no judgment, no wars, no killing in the name of God or country. In that world humanity would think of humanity's needs and provide for them. And at the end of the day, how wonderful it would be to watch the sun set, knowing each evening that friend is with friend, lover with lover, and families all together without the pain of separation.

In this spirit I simply say, "Namaste." I greet the God in everyone.

Suffering and Service

So many years have passed since death in the form of AIDS came early to many of my children, much too early. So many years have passed since the ache in our hearts made us one. So many memories remain. In those days when there were so few medicines, our ashrams together held fifteen to twenty memorials a week.

May we remember all those who lost their lives to AIDS. May we remember the struggle of those who were so dear to us.

Here at Kashi the ashes of our many dead fill our sacred Ganga, and in the quiet of the early morning hours one can feel the love and beauty of those *too many, too young, and too close to our hearts,* who rest beneath the still waters. I look toward our Ganga, where the ashes of so many rest, and I ask our beloved dead to teach us never to forget. I ask our Mother Kali to give us the strength to work and serve with hearts wide open.

AIDS is not over yet; it rages through Africa and India and, yes, even through our own United States. Indifference must never become a part of our lives, not for an instant.

How can we love so much and so well without burning out from our care-giving? We can go on only if we look at our work with gratefulness and know in our soul of souls that it is we who in serving are being served. Life flows through each one of us, and death touches us all. The living must be cared for, and the dead must be never forgotten.

Once more I look toward our Ganga, where the ashes of so many rest, and I ask our beloved dead to teach us never to forget that in their names we may care for a world hurt by AIDS.

Fear of Death

We hold to life by a thin thread, and at one time or another all of us contemplate our life, our future, and our death. Where there is life there is death, and death is everywhere in life, so it makes sense to live as fully as you can, being grateful for every day. Life is a blessing in itself, and if you can learn everything about it, there in life you will find the answer to death.

There are many kinds of death. One is the death of the things you do not need in your life. One at a time let those deaths occur. One by one let the burdens die. When there is finally the death of pride, the way will be open to reach God and Goddess.

The big secret of the universe is giving, no matter how you feel. The humblest of trees are the ones with the most fruit to give. They are so filled with fruit that they cannot help but bow.

The river of life is deep, yet it is bounded by the shores of death. I teach always of our Ganga being this river, flowing through all that live and breathe.

Can you let go of all that you think you want but do not need? Can you each day feel less anxious than before and more secure in the abundance of God's love? As you learn to swim in the river of life, always breathe with gratitude and love, and one day you will be able to approach the shores of death with no fear at all. And once you have arrived, you will find that you always knew what death is about.

But do you realize how hard it is to learn? That is because you are afraid to look at yourself too deeply, and that fear makes it hard to see the truth.

To fear death does nothing but bring stress to your life, but fears melt away as you live in your heart. The more you meditate and the more silent your mind becomes, the less fear can sink into your being. The more silent your mind, the louder your heart becomes. The louder your heart, the greater your life becomes. The greater your life, the more you can give others. The way to bring greatness to your life is to practice your dharma—your beliefs and duties—with awareness and, of course, with compassion.

For as long as you live, take each breath and use it well. As you breathe with awareness, you leave no dark shadows, only light and more light. Every breath becomes a blessing, and you will feel energized by the knowledge that life is, and can be, a brilliant triumph over death. Practice dying this day by living fully, and you can learn easily that death has a heart.

I have always said that death has a heart. I discovered this many years ago when I was meditating on Yama, the king of death. When Yama comes to greet you, will you be ready? Is there anything that you will want to change about yourself before you have this visitor? As you live your life, know that death is no more to be feared than birth. Know also that if you do not fear death, then you will never fear life. Remember that even Yama, death itself, will bow to the many forms of God, who are the guru, the paramaguru, the Mother Kali, and Lord Shiva, the reigning king of all.

If you have a heart filled full with love, fear has no place in your life, nor does pride. Pride is always the last to go. As long as pride is your master, it gets you into trouble, lifetime after lifetime, and leads you to repeat the same mistakes over and over. Sometimes pride comes disguised in the form of fear. If this is the case, then you must look deeply into your heart and understand your fears. The Mother has always been here for you. Is it pride that makes you forget this? Recognize pride before another lifetime passes you by.

With the death of pride comes the death of ego. When the ego dies, you rejoice in the awareness of the eternal Self, the real you, which floats above life and death. The truth of life and death is taught to you in the silence of your own heart. The more still you become, the greater you are able to hear all you need to know in order to live a spiritual life, in order to gain the insight of Self-knowledge.

Closed Heart, Closed Mind

When you are governed by ignorance, it affects the mind, body, and soul. You are affected in every part of your personality. Ignorance gives birth to judgment, judgment gives birth to anger, and anger brings pain to you and the ones you love. Where there is no openness of the heart, there is no love for God or yourself or others. In the face of this conflict and pain, a closed heart first withers and then becomes dry. When the heart is crippled, the mind becomes agitated by dissatisfaction, resentment, and revenge.

When you allow yourself to understand how much you are loved by God, the smaller you begins to disappear. You are less afraid to show your own vulnerability and you become more able to endure other people's criticism or anger without taking it so personally. A devotee whose heart remains open no matter what is going on in life is indeed dear to the Mother. No matter what the conditions are, the one whose heart is open always feels the soft breath of springtime.

The journey to God must be taken with an open heart and an open mind. On this journey, the seeker turns totally to the God within and the guru within. Resting at the feet of the guru in the heart, the seeker has no home in the world of duality but is always in the oneness of God. The seeker whose heart is open is endowed with steady understanding and devotion.

Be sensitive toward your own spiritual moments. When you sit in meditation, let all the love in your heart freely unfold through a feeling of fullness that you never felt before. This is the inter-faith way.

Understand how important it is to be open and to welcome every-one and everyone's beliefs. Become a true disciple of the formless God with all the love in your heart, and know that the formless God is indeed universal—the interfaith God and Goddess of all peoples. Discover your relationship with all peoples, and know that this love is the greatest of healers. Whatever God you wor-ship, whatever path you follow, you must understand that God is a lover of every soul. There is no single way that is perfect. All ways are perfect if they are God's ways.

A Poisonous Garland

Thoughts can be like flowers strung in a garland, and when they are thoughts of love and compassion, the garland shows off your beauty. But when they are thoughts of resentment and revenge, the garland becomes a snare that closes in on you like a circle of misery.

A complaint I often hear is that many of you are not understood by the people around you. But the people who don't understand can play a part in your spiritual growth as well. Every rose has its thorns, yet the beauty of the rose is always there, isn't it?

If unfair criticism comes your way, feel sorry for the person who has nothing better to do than to criticize. You need to know that blackness always falls back on blackness; those who would hurt you end up hurting themselves.

Even though many people seek revenge when they feel hurt, revenge can never appease them. They are drawn into seeking still more vengeance without growing toward the light of God.

Do not let this happen to you! If you saw that someone was hurt deeply by your vicious actions, would that make you a happier person? Hatred for one being grows into hatred for others, and when you hate in this way, a deep fear is released in your being. The fear is that perhaps you hate yourself.

When people try to cast their negative thoughts on you, pay no attention. Always be drawn to the positive. When you begin to know the true you, you outgrow fear and pride and pettiness. By knowing yourself you get to know others. With this knowledge you can feel the light of God surround you, and so can they. Think of the Mother's love, and feel a huge rush of caring. There is no need to want to inflict pain on others. There is every need to want to reach out to them in love.

By bringing discipline to your heart and continuing in that discipline, you will be able to discern the difference between qualities coming from the ego-mind or the God-heart. Never burden yourself with thoughts of what you should have done. Do not even burden yourself with uncertainty over what you should do. Nothing good will come of that, only confusion, anger, and despair.

So, what should you do?

First, balance the mind and soothe the heart by remembering God. Divine surrender is just putting your will in her hands, nothing more. Instead of disastrous thoughts of resentment and hatred, which will only poison your life, you—the spiritual seeker—can fill yourself with thoughts of nature, flowers, sky, children, guru, love, and God. When you do this, the mental impurities that create bad karma cannot stick to your soul and follow you around from lifetime to lifetime.

Then bring yourself into the moment by doing good. It does not cost you anything to say "I love you" to someone if you mean it. It does that person good, and you will find your own heart floating with love. The power of divine grace will miraculously lead you to a place of healing of others and yourself.

All it asks of you is complete honesty. Be free of delusion and malice, and you can make no mistake.

You

As the world continues to slide into one war after another and there is constant anxiety all around, watch out for flare-ups of self-doubt and unworthiness. No matter how much negativity surrounds you, you must not let your ego take your attention away from the beautiful essence of who you are.

Do not make room for negativity. Do not let anything take you off guard. Simply allow anxiety to drift away like a cloud as you watch the breath and return to the abiding calm of the moment.

Enjoy the perfection of the moment—your perfection and worthiness. Your birthright is to be happy and free. Who are you to take that away from you?

If you want to grow spiritually, you must concentrate with awareness on every aspect of your life. See where it is expanding or contracting. If you see it contracting, pulling in on itself, correct this in your mind by bringing in a new, expansive attitude. If you feel your life is just going nowhere, focus your attention on the breath and see where you are stuck. Then breathing in and out, unblock the *chakra* which is keeping you from God. It is a simple matter of developing spiritual sensitivity.

For example, if you feel that you have no control over your anger, you need to open your heart chakra, for this is the center of love. Close your eyes and visualize your awareness spreading through your life as spiritual wakefulness. Try to identify with your open heart and not with a closed mind. Then open your eyes to a sense of love all around you. The more you recognize your own spiritual nature, the more you will recognize the spirituality in everyone else.

The ego does not give up easily. Sometimes in your time of quiet, when you sit in the stillness, that which is within you gets stirred up and rises to the surface. It is not always pretty. That which is disturbing belongs to the mind and its thoughts of who you think you are. Let it pass, and let the ideas that are born of the heart replace the ideas that are born of the mind.

There is brittleness in the mind-thoughts and flexibility and softness in the heart-thoughts.

The mind comes in whenever you feel any kind of negativity. As you walk toward the negativity, you become something you are not. This is the mind of the ego. Fearful thoughts and angry thoughts are filled with emptiness and can lead to actions that hurt. They have no home within your being. Explore your ego-thoughts, then let them go to the cremation grounds of Mother Kali. When you can assert the knowing that has always been in you, you will understand that there is something sacred about what you always have known. This knowing is free of self-deception. Do not ignore your own truth.

When you sense the sunlight outside but fail to step out of your door, then you are wasting the sun's light.

When you feel the warmth of the sun on your brow but fail to greet it with gratitude, then again you are wasting the sun's light.

If you choose to live in the gloomy dampness of self-pity and confine your heart to the limits of the ego-room where you've locked yourself in, you have only yourself to blame.

Whenever you choose to, you can step out of the darkness of suffering and misery that you've made for yourself. Your self-inflicted sufferings are created by ego and dispelled by grace. Go toward the grace of God every day of your life. Go toward the sunlight of grace.

You—Again

You have heard me speak many times of your beauty. "What beauty?" you ask. How many times do I have to tell you? I tell you now to sit quietly and look into the stillness for your own beauty. In the depth of meditation, the mind lies still. Outside of meditation the mind is never truly still but scattered in many ways because of desires, anger, and fears.

Still, many people are afraid to be alone with themselves and therefore fear meditation. They fear because they are afraid of getting to know themselves, afraid of seeing something they may not like. They do not know that anything about themselves can be changed if they choose to change it. They do not know that their inner essence is already perfect and pure.

You do not see your own beauty when you allow yourself to feel empty or sad, when you allow the mind to keep wandering, when you cannot concentrate on the awareness that you are never apart from the Mother in all her splendor.

You do not see your own beauty when you ache to feel the Goddess touching your soul, forgetting that you already are with her day and night, night and day.

You do not see your own beauty when you do not let everything in your life remind you of her love.

Look at your lower self, your troublesome self, which is ruled by the restlessness of the body and the mind and the ego. Look carefully and see what you want to change. Be conscious in dealing with your mind. If you see that your ego is leading you on, take a moment to breathe in and out of your heart. Take time to find the nectar of God within your own heart.

The human tragedy is how easily you forget to live in your own wonderful awareness.

With a deep breath pull the lower, smaller self into the joy of the higher Self. Let yourself be drawn in, and at the same time give up whatever you do not need. Let it all be dissolved in your connectedness to God the Mother. Do not be afraid to trust that the Mother Kali, who is blacker than black, will consume all the negativity.

Complete trust in God will come only when you fully trust your own heart, because your heart is where you will find your God, who is your higher Self. You will recognize your own beauty in your higher Self.

To be on a spiritual journey is also to give to others. There is a great beauty in gentleness and kindness, but sometimes it is difficult to awaken such feelings inside you without fear of rejection. Never be afraid to expose a moment of love, but let it flow like a river from your heart. Once started, the flowing never stops. Even though another person may reject you, know that the Mother never will. Approach her and break through all your fears. Learn to let love in, and make your life complete by loving who you truly are. You are the one that God the Mother loves just as you are.

Treat others with dignity, and you will find dignity within yourself. Be ever mindful that having a body gives you a vehicle and living on earth gives you an opportunity to serve others in many ways. Do not be limited in your love, but give freely and watch how love flows through you and touches other lives.

Once you taste the bliss of God for yourself, you will want it for everyone. Your open heart, like a lotus blossom, is not subject to the smallness of your lower self but blooms in the full beauty of love that knows no bounds.

It's Up to You

If you want to become who you truly are, this is the time to act with full devotion and integrity. This change can happen only if you are ready and willing.

When you feel alone in the world, just think: how can you be lonely when the Mother is always with you? She who created you and the trees and flowers and beautiful moments is just a breath away. Why do you feel lonely?

If times are hard, times will change. If you sit for a little while every day and meditate on love, you can attune your own little mind to the universal mind, which is the divine Oneness.

When your mind is attuned to the Mother, who is your true and only Self, how can there be room in your life for loneliness? You will be finding the place that you have sought for so long, the place that is not the isolation of your body and personality.

Will you heed the call of the Mother and love yourself? Know that God rejects no one and accepts everyone. Who are you, then, to reject God or another human being? In life you are free to make many choices. Make the choice to live fully in the life of the spirit, always open to the presence of the Mother in her many forms.

This day decide to be productive spiritually. Do not create moments of delay. Do not create moments of divisiveness. Do not cling to thoughts of divisiveness. Instead, think of knowing the true Self.

Without unleashing the flow of shakti, the power of knowledge, you cannot know yourself fully. Each time you sit with awareness, you penetrate the higher consciousness, yet you must do this with all your heart and soul.

To experience the Mother within you, you need to have her on your mind and in your heart constantly. Repeat to yourself constantly the words, "Mother is in me," and after a while you will feel and hear the inner words, "I am in you." There is no telling how long this may take; just keep going.

Place your goals in front of you, not too high and not too low. If you want to hit the target, go slowly and surely. There is nothing that you cannot accomplish. Even if there is frustration or failure along the way, know in your heart of hearts that you can conquer any obstacle. The universal stream of spiritual victory, *jaya*, is in you. True victory is mastery over the senses and mastery over the moment. Even small goals bring victory, and each small victory brings you one step closer to the goal.

What are your dreams? What goals do you pursue? In order to have a real and lasting joy you must come to understand your own divine essence. Perhaps you have reached many of your goals without even knowing it. It takes time and love to understand yourself, yet it is definitely worth it. When you get to know yourself, you will begin truly to know others. When you see your own beauty, which means recognizing God within yourself, you will very easily see the beauty of others, and see God in them. This love can have no limits.

Love is the newness of each new dawn that the Mother Usha brings as a gift. Show your gratitude by being honest and simple in your day. As you put one foot in front of the other, remember to trust in the Mother who sustains you. Remember what is truly important and try hard not to reach for something that may not really matter.

If pain and anger come up, what will you do? You must be like the sages, searching in your heart for the wisdom of love. Be joyful in your pursuit, and you will learn how not to be a captive of your own anger.

Be neither too eager nor too slow, but go steadily toward your goals. Look inertia in the face and conquer it. Little by little you will find your own shakti, your own creativity. Be of service to the people around you, and as the joys of selflessness reveal themselves, see how much more easily your goals are attained. Let this vision lead you beyond the little self and into the full-blown Self of knowledge, where you will be detached and joyous.

You hold the key to success in opening and keeping open your spiritual heart. First, be enthusiastic in your meditation; through steady practice you will become more and more in harmony with your heart. Then let all your beautiful qualities unfold layer by layer as you live your life on the spiritual path, the harmonious interfaith path that rejects no one and respects all.

Ask the great god Ganesha to remove all obstacles on your path to liberation. He will show you how to develop harmony between your thoughts, words, and deeds.

Of course, the mind does not become purified overnight. You will have to work at it. Give no attention to your negative thoughts except to offer them to Mother Kali. Remain as if you were a detached witness to your attachments, and take note how fast they will fly away.

Learn the harmonious art of giving to others, and know that this is the secret of an open heart. Educate your heart in the beauty of love and compassion, and promote good karmas in your day-to-day living. When you breathe in and out of your heart, give your thoughts up to love. Darkness will vanish even as harmony with the universe dawns, and you will be led, ever so gently, toward spiritual victory, toward the realization of the divine Self.

INTERLUDE

The Divine Mother

DURGA

Sometimes as I sit very quietly in the early dawn, I ask if the true nature of God is beyond human comprehension, and the answer is, the true nature of God the Mother is her children's hearts.

To know you are a child of the Mother Durga in all her many forms, this in itself is bliss! All things are the image of the Mother. She has her center everywhere, because she lives in every heart.

If you sit very quietly in the early dawn, you can hear the Mother beckoning. Listen to her call you and resolve to meet yourself, your real Self, in your heart of hearts without any more delay. The breath can take you there, and by sitting there with the Mother, worshiping her and meditating on her, you fall more and more in love, and you want the Mother's love to flow throughout the world. With the Mother's name always on your lips and breath, you will want these blissful moments for everyone.

Enjoy your life on the spiritual path, and remember always to share this sweetness with all you come across. There is nothing else on the face of this earth to which the Mother's love can be compared. Her love is boundless and unconditional, and she wants you, her child, to share it with all your sisters and brothers. Be ever united with her love, and with your heart wide open, embrace everyone in acceptance, just as she embraces all her children all over the world.

My chelas, the Mother is beckoning to you to go beyond your mind and body and to venture into your true being. She is beckoning to you to be a yogi, to be awake in self-awareness.

You can choose to hear her call. She is calling you to sit in the place of wisdom in the heart, at the feet of God, where you can learn how to turn away from all your boundaries and know you are free. Begin this very day to consume all restrictions: the ones that you were born with and the ones that you continuously place upon yourself. In your meditations let your awareness fly with the freedom of an eagle.

To awaken this freedom within yourself, just remember without doubt that the Mother in two of her strongest forms, Durga and Kali, will always come to your rescue. Focus your awareness on Mother Durga's shining might. She is the fiercely protective Mother and warrior goddess. It is said that the Mother Kali springs from Durga's forehead in time of need. A chela needs only to call on Shri Durga in order to feel Mother Kali's presence as well.

Either or both will come, armed with a vast array of weapons. These are symbols of the Divine Mother's powers to destroy darkness and evil. These are, in fact, the powers of your own higher mind and open heart. By calling on the Mother in her powerful forms, you awaken within yourself the great ability to overcome spiritual darkness and limitation. You are never alone and never need to feel alone upon this earth.

KALI

The supreme Mother can be reached by all her children according to their own religions and paths. The divine Mother Kali reveals herself in many forms from gentle to fierce. Choose the one you are most comfortable with and say, "This day, my Mother, my God, I want to spend with you, doing nothing by my own will, but only thinking of you and following your direction." Try this, and get used to communicating freely with her.

As Kali Ma, though she is dark, she removes darkness. She who removes negativity is always just a breath away, no more than that. Call on her and know that it is she who breathes through you. She is with you in your heart and will bestow comfort and joy.

Visualize yourself, the Kali yogi, seated in the Mother's heart, even as she sits between the sun and the moon. Now combine their lights in the fire of *prema*, the fire of divine love. This is no ordinary love, but an all-consuming devotion. Offer any duality in your heart—any sense of separation or loneliness or limitation—to the blazing fire of the Mother's love and ask her to take you into the Oneness.

It does not matter who you are, you are loved by the Mother Kali. Know that you are blessed to be alive and in a body. When you feel that you are one with the universal Mother of many names and forms, then you can feel that you are one with everyone and everything on this earth and in the heavens. The Mother is interwoven in you and is the support of all.

Whomever you see, whomever you serve, know that they too are blessed to be alive and in a body. Whatever you do this day, know that you are in the Mother and that she is in you.

GANGA

The river Ganga is ancient and sacred to all Hindus. Flowing from heaven, her mighty descent is tamed by Lord Shiva himself, who catches her in his matted locks. She then takes on the physical form of all the oceans and lakes, ponds and rivers, and flows gently and sweetly upon the earth, purifying all she touches.

You can feel any holy river as Mother Ganga. The waters of rivers all over the world flow and cascade with her shakti. Mother Ganga can be called upon whenever you bathe or shower or wash your face or use water in any way. Just call on her, and she will make herself known. When you begin to understand that *puja* (worship) can be done at any moment when water is used, you have for yourself a portable altar. As the water in your sink touches your hands, imagine that they are in the Ganga. Her holy waters can bless you like no other, at any given moment. At any time, you can tune in to the flowing Mother and trust that being in her presence will allow your heart to open more and more. Mentally you can swim in the Ganga with your hearts filled with joy. Call out her name—"Jai Ganga Ma Ki Jai!"—over and over again. Whenever you feel lost or unsure, bring your mind back to the Ganga, and she will be with you. Trust yourself, and make a commitment to your heart that you will trust yourself even more.

As the current of a river can wash away obstructions, the all- purifying Ganga, flowing through your awareness, will show you new ways to let go of attachments which are thick and solid. The Ganga, tumbling in a mighty cascade from heaven and tamed by Lord Shiva's locks, flows gently and purifies all she touches. The Mother Ganga is the great puri-fier, flowing through every heart.

Our Baba told me long ago that we all can be the bearer of the Mother Ganga, the bearers of the divine Shakti. My chelas, does this not make us all Shiva? How many times do you speak of the greatness of God, yet fail to see the greatness of yourselves? It is time to give up all unworthi-ness, to vanquish all your fears and examine your beautiful heart, bathed in the purifying waters of the Ganga. Let her, the Mother, wash away all that which you do not need, and I promise that divinity will make itself known to your heart.

Every day, be nourished and purified by the Ganga's holy waters, and let love flow from your heart like a refreshing spring.

SHAKTI

Shakti is God's own creative power and the energy that keeps the whole universe alive. When personified, she is Shakti, that aspect of the Divine Mother who gives birth to the universe, nurtures all existence, and draws everything back to herself. The word shakti, when used in a general sense, means that same power or energy, just not in a personal sense.

Shakti flows through the heart of every being, and so you too have the ability deep within yourself to make things happen. You can be aware of this by being in the moment all day long and feeling the powerful stillness of the Mother in your heart. When dedicated to meditation and yoga and good deeds, the body and mind work in perfect harmony. When you allow your mind to return to the source of all things— shakti— this same shakti will fill your life with bliss and joy.

Love is the essential ingredient to attune yourself to Shakti, for she is the nurturing power throughout creation. The body, mind, and soul are all nourished by the beauty of shakti that you can pass on to others through your acts of love and compassion. There is a limitless ocean of love in you, and your actions can be a shining example of who you are. Be radiant today, knowing that to the Mother in any of her many forms, you are a precious jewel.

The important part of this teaching is not to sit still and just wish for whatever you want. You must look inside yourself and find ways to serve humanity as well as yourself.

How do you serve yourself? One way is to put this teaching to use with everything you have. Breathe deeply, now and whenever you think of it, and feel the sacred current of shakti flowing through you. In other words, overcome inertia this very moment. Shakti—divine energy as the Mother—begets shakti, the divine force as you consciously put it into action. Let the Divine Mother's light of understanding reveal to you who you truly are. Let it be your guide.

Do not waste your shakti on things which serve no one, not even yourselves. When your behavior becomes self-destructive and you feel yourself falling by the wayside, let your own higher awareness lead you to make the right choices. Such choices will bring you, my chelas, closer to seeing the beauty of your own heart and the beauty in every heart.

Use the past well. Don't become stuck in what was, but know that love is what *is*, and *what is* is the heart of now. Once you have tasted the nectar of the Mother's love, there is no turning back. It pulls you deep into her universal essence. As a child grows in its mother's womb, you grow spiritually in the Mother's universal womb, as her rhythm of life pulsates in your heart, as your blood circulates like the holy waters of the Ganga, as the shakti of infinite love breathes through every cell of your body. Feel it within you; it has always been. It is only you who have forgotten.

PART THREE
The Way

Be Awakened

This day and every day, when you awaken, you have the opportunity to awaken to your God-nature, to awaken to the divine love that flows within you every moment. Your holiness is apparent to your guru or spiritual teacher. Now it is time for it to be apparent to you, for you to see who you really are. Now is the time for you to recognize all your blessings and be in a state of reverence.

Everything you do can be sacred and blessed if you do it with awareness and love. It is the divine intelligence within your heart that keeps you in your heart and guides you, if you are quiet enough, to live as one who is always awake. When you turn to the Mother, she will allow you to walk through life freely and purely, untouched by things of the world, yet living in the world. When you turn to the Mother in any form, all separation ends. You become part of the Mother's heart. You become part of her grace.

Look around you and feel how much you are blessed. Breathe deeply and feel the love that is yours to have forever. Awaken the sleeping heart and be in touch with the Divine Mother in your heart of hearts. Breathe in gratitude and send the gratitude out to the world. As you exhale, gratitude turns to love. Do this every day, and be awakened.

The Power of Silence

Only a silent mind can live a full life.

Only a silent mind can feel the silent heart.

Only a silent mind can hear the sound of the Mother's voice.

Only a silent mind can find the purpose of those words.

Only a silent mind can receive the knowledge of reality.

Do not sacrifice action for stillness, and do not sacrifice stillness for action, but allow all actions to flow from that silent space of love and joy. When the mind is still, your life becomes energetic. But when the mind is filled with fear, you can hardly be still. The scattered mind finds a scattered life.

Be gentle in your meditation and find the true you in the stillness of your heart. Silence is the grace of God, which you give yourself. If you are having difficulty meditating, just sit and start to count backwards from one thousand. Try it. Just don't get impatient. If you lose your place, just start again—and again—and again.

Keeping in mind that God the Mother and God the Father always love you, breathe in the experience of God-love. As you breathe in, feel the warmth of love in your chest. Feel the chest expand and expand. As you live in the here and now, feel love intensely in the moment. Now let out the breath with purpose. In other words, breathe out love for world peace or kindness or compassion for everyone or for someone special.

When you observe the breath in this way, you become aware that there are many treasures in the mystical heart. There is the action of breathing love that can keep you going when things are not going quite right. There is a vibration of love that comes to you in the silence of your heart. The vibration of love touches upon the unknown and encompasses all the wisdom of God. Nothing is as powerful as the vibration of love. Anger cannot live in the same place as love, so why not give love a chance? You have only to make space for this vibration. It will free you from personal bondage.

Ordinarily the mind holds on to the ego-words that constantly run through it. Often it is worried and anxious. By watching the breath, you still the mind. With practice you will come to recognize and welcome this state of stillness. The silent mind is the fire that burns the ego. When the ego is reduced to ash, the heart knows no separation but only harmony with God the Mother and God the Father. This harmony also brings well-being to the body.

The stillness of meditation brings peace, because it is free of intrusive thoughts. It is not so difficult to let go of the mind when the silence is thick and juicy. Breathe in these moments and give them your full awareness. The serenity you seek will come with the stillness. That stillness is awareness, and awareness allows all moments to be stretched.

Deep within your soul of souls, there is a memory of you and God. It is there. You only have to discover your own reality, which has nothing to do with anything external. Your reality is God's reality. Your reality is pure and has no gender. Your reality is bliss. The guru teaches you how to touch the source of life within your own heart and to drink fully. Let stillness come upon you.

Spare time each day for the joy of conversing silently with God. When meditation comes to have a steady place in your life, your life itself makes more time for you to meditate. Meditation becomes something that you look forward to, because it is silent, still, and joyful. It is the stream of shakti, the power of consciousness, flowing like the holy Ganga herself. This stillness is something you can remember if you are simply quiet enough. Meditation is the power of stillness, and stillness in meditation brings stillness in life.

As you sit in meditation, you begin to understand what meditation really is. It is all about stilling the mind and feeling the heart. In this state, holiness can be perceived through the feelings of the heart and the thoughts of a quiet mind drawn to God. Appreciation and gratitude will bring an inner awakening and transform you.

Discover for yourself your true inner beauty. And if you make mistakes this day, walk on tall and strong and learn from your mistakes.

When the world is at war and humanity has gotten off the track, it is important for you to be on the track of peace, to feel peace in every part of your being. To discover the wholeness of your reality is to discover the wholeness of everyone on earth.

Create a space of grace for you to sit in every day. Love to love. Love to see the goodness in others. Enjoy bringing love to all you meet. Sometimes it is just a smile that will light up the face and heart of a stranger. Give love away freely and feel more and more love come in.

When your mind is still, you begin to have fleeting moments of who you truly are. As you sit for longer and longer periods, deep sincerity, love of the moment, and joy in life burst forth, and there comes a moment when this joy must be shared with others. There is a language of love and life that the true mystic perceives. Like drops of nectar, its words will sweeten your tongue. Love bursts through the heart, and with it comes a deep desire to bring comfort to those in need.

In the heart of silence, the mind can no longer deceive you. The silent heart knows what needs to be accomplished. You only need to be still in your meditation to hear the infinite voice within you speak and guide your actions. It will tell you to give up your insecurities and feelings of unworthiness. It will tell you to be aware of your own boundlessness and your own perfection. Sit in stillness and know you are whole in this moment and every moment. Allow your heart to receive love and allow yourself to give love freely. Be free of the past and learn to live in the moment of love and grace.

The heart has a huge capacity for love, love that can be breathed in all day long. As your heart grows warm with the thought of God's love, you spread this warmth to others. You find that you want to make others happy. You will feel almost as if you have a responsibility to be still, to be silent and aware, to be full and compassionate. A few moments of this God-like stillness bring many blessings that you can impart to others. The more you serve others, the more bliss of God you know, because the more you serve others, the more you are serving God. You cannot deny love, or you would be denying your own existence.

When you become really quiet, and this indeed takes practice, you enter into the timelessness of the Mother. As long as you live listening to the Mother's voice in your heart of hearts, you will not get caught in illusion. You will not violate your own perfection by thinking you are less than who you truly are.

It only takes a silent mind to let you know.

Attuning the Mind

The nature of the God-mind is very different from that of the worldly mind. Yet all minds are connected to each other.

Everyone in the world shares a common spirit, but many choose to ignore the God spirit and go their own ways, driven on by the wants and fears and hopes of the worldly ego. Others, who do not ignore the God spirit, look for the company of spiritually-minded seekers and enjoy being in tune with them and with the guru or teacher of their choice. In that environment a certain kind of spirituality enters into all of those who breathe and sing and worship and meditate together.

When you are constantly distracted on your path to God, you must ask the Mother to bring your attention back to the moment. The straying ego-mind is obvious once you are taught to recognize it. You can consume its illusion and enter into reality if your heart is open. There is no need for you to be deluded by the external appearances that you take for reality.

Ask your heart about reality. All the wisdom you need is in your God-heart. When you constantly perform *samyama* (steady, intense concentration), you gain insight into whatever you have focused on. The higher mind envelops a thought and brings this thought to the heart in the split second of eternity. Then when you face a difficult situation, you will not react rashly but instead save yourself and others a great deal of pain and suffering. There is great restraining power in the wisdom of the heart.

Here is a good meditation for the early dawn, or any time you need to focus:

Close your eyes and bring all the shakti that is in you and around you to your heart, and then with the breath raise the shakti up to your third eye, the point between the eyebrows.

Think about what you have to be focused on.

Concentrate now on the chakra between the eyebrows, and see its light travel upward and through the crown chakra at the top of the head.

Next, breathe light into the space of your spiritual heart and feel the wonder of God-bliss.

Breathe the light out into the world, and send its bliss to others.

Always let the light of the third eye purify the intellect and flood the heart with love. When you perform samyama on the third eye, this chakra begins to pulsate with joy, and when the third eye opens, the mysteries of spiritual life unfold.

Always identify with the light of the Self and never with the darkness of the mind. In the light of the Goddess nothing can be hidden or obscure. She, the Mother, penetrates all the layers that hide your true nature, which is love. Stay in your heart and bring love to everyone you meet. Do not succumb to your wandering thoughts, but be diligent in your pursuits. It takes great devotion and dedication to a spiritual life to keep focused while in the world, but the rewards are great.

When you can focus, there will be less procrastination, less unhappiness, and less of the feeling that there are burdens on your back. With love and concentration, everything comes into proper focus. This spiritual exercise will bring you more clarity than you can imagine.

Right Action

When you sit in meditation, you are able to find your own inner strength. This inner strength will grow as you find the courage never to waver from your spiritual path. When you learn not to waver, then you become ready to translate your own inner strength into right action.

Right action means never taking advantage of another human being and always being there for others. We are all related to one other. We are one. It is when we forget that we are one that we become discontented with our lives and enter into pain and sometimes cause harm to others.

If this should happen, be silent and receive the Mother's divine energy, her shakti. Silence is not passive. Silence is energetic. Silence is productive. This silence of shakti allows you to embrace life and to live fully and do the right thing at all times. Let the lotus of your loving heart unfold in the silent moment of the Mother.

You may think that you do not know what is right and what is not, yet I assure you that you do. You can tell what is false and what is true. Falseness cripples your mind and your heart. Truth opens your heart and floods the dryness with joy. In fact, true joy and happiness cannot be found outside of your heart, so follow your heart in all that you do.

As you sit more and more in meditation, you will be less and less able to deceive yourself with negative thoughts. Instead, you will be in awe. As you build on your love for God, you will feel your love grow like a beautiful garden. Right action will grow in your garden from the seeds you have sown yourself. As you serve and love others, happiness grows like the tree of life within you, each day growing mightier. Once this process has started there is no stopping.

From this day on, be responsible for your actions. Make no excuses, and blame no one else if your day does not go as you want it to go. Offer everything to the Mother. She will take whatever you offer her with devotion, and through devotion you will learn to live every moment well.

Growing Strong

When you begin the path of meditation, you are on the path to perfection. Little by little, day by day, meditation brings your life into balance. Each time you stop the mind by meditating on the heart chakra, you get a little stronger. You develop will power and discipline. Through repeated practice you learn to shake off any weakness and to stop wasting your power, your shakti, on worthless thoughts.

It is important to abstain from any type of negative thinking. When dark thoughts come into play, just breathe into your heart and remember the Mother's love. Repeat that thought over and over like a mantra. This will help you to develop a broad understanding of how to be disciplined in all aspects of your daily life. It takes practice and perseverance.

Sometimes when you least realize it, your will begins to weaken. You find that you begin to sabotage your own efforts to meditate and to feel joy. Again I say it takes practice and perseverance. The more you develop, the more you evolve toward God the Mother and God the Father. Surrender to God within your heart; then God's will becomes your will and your will becomes God's will. There is immense joy in this way of thinking and living. It lets you go forward and pursue your goals without anxiety or fear to weaken your resolve.

The poet Ramprasad sang of Mother Kali's glory on the battlefield. Become a spiritual warrior and feel the Mother leading you on your path. Be courageous. To be a spiritual warrior means to conquer everything about yourself that you do not like.

The Mother's power, shakti, is always on the move. When you stop yourself from receiving shakti by not liking yourself, then you are short-changing your very being. The less you like your-self, the less you like others. The instant you want to become someone else, you lose the value of who you are.

This moment take all concepts of who you would like to be and throw them into Mother Kali's fire. Now you are free to start again. This time listen carefully to her who dwells in your heart and know who you truly are.

The more you like yourself, the more you like others. It is when you judge others that you get off balance. Always remember that love is the strongest shakti you can experience. As you make progress in communicating with Mother Kali, your whole world changes. You become a part of her by greater and greater degrees, and you gain so much room in your heart to receive love and to give love.

There is nothing more filled with love than being aware. Aware-ness brings the moment into play. Through awareness you learn to play in the moment. Be strong this moment, and always, in the simple beauty of your own perfection.

Who Is a Yogi?

With a quiet mind you can rule your own life and find the peace of heart that is already there. A true yogi is someone who has withdrawn the senses as a turtle withdraws its limbs and rests firm in the wisdom of the heart. By concentrating upon the heart, the yogi brings the mind under control and is no longer its slave.

Who is a yogi? Anyone who knowingly spends time with the God of his or her choice. It is as simple as that. As the love in the heart overcomes the thoughts of the mind, the senses become completely controlled. Even if this lasts only a split second, it can bring great joy.

The God of your choice is whichever one you love and trust and worship. All gods and goddesses represent the goodness in all of us. All will lead you to the place of deep merging within your heart.

The state of yoga, or union, is a personal relationship between you and your God, between you and your higher Self. In yoga you constantly feel that power in all your movements, actions, and thoughts. When this power is known internally, it leaves a glow of divinity in you.

As the *asanas* (yoga postures) are practiced with awareness and attention is paid to the breath flowing quietly in and out, the gentle fire of love ignites in the heart and spreads throughout the body. Peace without distraction arises in your being. You discover that you care for one another, and you find your inner strength to care even more, especially in time of crisis.

When you care for one another, you are caring for God in another person. Your acts of caring become worship of God. Where there is love, there is movement, and the joy of love, like the breath, flows ever inward and outward and becomes your complete state of being.

Looking Inward

As you sit quietly, watch your chest rise and fall with the breath. Watch your whole being grow calm as you enter into the heart-space of love and detachment. Look within this very moment, and feel the great space of freedom that is yours to have.

As you go deeper and deeper inside, you begin to find bright areas that you never thought existed. Where you thought darkness dwelt and depression hung on, there is light now. Your meditations and the blessings of the guru have driven all darkness away.

In this light you have a greater ability now than ever before to see the greatness that you are. Every day practice deeper and deeper introspection, and you will know your own strength of spirit. You will find that you are equipped to handle any situation that comes your way. You only have to understand how much you have learned and changed within yourself.

When all your negative expressions of self begin to fade away and you see how wonderfully positive you can be, then your life grows lighter in every way possible. You can live going forward and never looking back. Keep moving toward the light. If you are burdened with old hurts, know that forgiveness is the best balm to remove them. Through forgiveness simply let them go.

Through looking inward you will discover new energies that will help you to live your life to the fullest degree. Looking inward changes how you look outward. With a new outlook, feel free to inspire yourself in any way to live a God-filled life. Change what you want to change about yourself and love the rest. In fact, love even what you want to change, and shed all feelings of negativity. A positive frame of mind will make it easier to change. Learn to love even the small things about yourself, and let your true self begin to bloom.

Practice, Practice, Practice

Sadhana, the word for spiritual practice, means never giving up on yourself. The great secret in spiritual life is practice—repeated effort, trying over and over to become what you truly want to become, what you truly are. If you practice being kind, you become kind. When your daily life is permeated with the spirit of love, you become this spirit of love. Practice remembering God and you become established in divine love.

As you fall more and more in love, the unstable, fleeting conditions of life begin to fade into the steady light of loving God. Why, then, should you let your mind distract your heart away from this joy?

For the vast majority of souls, spiritual success does not come in a sudden blast of higher consciousness. Almost all seekers have to work at it. You must sustain your effort in meditation, and as you do, you learn to enjoy your time alone with your God. This brings a change to your unconscious mind and to your conscious mind as well. You will learn to melt the difference between your lower self and your higher Self.

Know that love is the language of the heart and that the heart must stay wide open for bliss to flow through it.

Through meditation all answers are yours before questions even arise, because the mysteries of creation are known to your heart. Consciously bring the Mother to her abode in your heart cave. This fulfillment of love in the heart surpasses anything of the earth. In this Mother's love there is no need to seek perfection. You are perfect as you are now. Sadhana will take you to this knowledge.

And so--make this morning count, make this afternoon count, make this night count. Do not procrastinate for a single day. Do not let anything get in your way of approaching God, whether through yoga or prayer or meditation or any other form of spiritual practice.

Throughout the day, whenever the thought arises, take deep and wonderful breaths into the pit of your belly, and let out all the tension. Dissolve any conflict or separation that keeps you from your inner beauty. Find an impeccable quality within yourself, and dissolve the image of failure.

Be aware of what you want to get rid of in your life and see how much freer you feel. No matter what happens, make this day a bright day by keeping that sense of freedom close to you as your constant inspiration. Make this your practice.

Meditation

Have you ever sat quietly and listened to your own heartbeat? Listening to your heart takes you from external chaos to the space within, where God the Mother reveals herself in moments of quiet. Getting into this habit of deep listening will allow you eventually to recognize the Mother even outside in the world of chaos.

As you sit and listen, you begin to trust your own intuitive feelings that come from the heart. The more you trust your intuition, the fewer mistakes you make in your life and the lives of others. You have the ability to take care of your problems. To find the answers, you need only to listen in the stillness of meditation. When you get in touch with your intuition, you learn how to live in harmony. Then, coming out of the silence, you find that life is like a huge orchestra. As you watch the conductor, God the Mother, and attune yourself, you will find yourself in harmony with others. You will know how to express your individual thoughts, feelings, and love in the proper way. As you sit in meditation, the intuition of who you are bursts forth in your own expression of knowledge and wisdom, and that wisdom of the open heart becomes your own source of strength.

To begin your practice, be quiet for a short time each day, and take a moment and examine your life and your priorities. You will be reminded of your relationship with God, of putting God the Mother and God the Father first in your life, then placing God's children next. If you put love first, after that all else will be taken care of. You will learn the spiritual secret of transcending activity, and your whole life will change.

When you stimulate the heart through meditation on love, a vitality flows through you to others and makes apparent the joy and bliss and freedom in God.

Repeated effort in meditating will remove the impressions left on the mind by your attachments. Even if you want to retrieve them, you can't, because the heart will be filled with a love so deep that all past attachments are drowned. The heart will then reflect only on the infinite splendor of the Absolute. Keep your heart always immersed in this union with God.

During meditation you seek to recapture the silence that is naturally yours, the silence where you learn to be alone with God.

Sometimes the noise of your thoughts will get in the way. If you have negative thoughts, or any thoughts other than those of God within, let them drift away like clouds.

The mind is just like a child: if you yell at it, it will do what it wants. So, do not get upset, but be kind to your thoughts and simply watch them drift away. Soon you will welcome the silence and know that silence is just another form of love.

It is important to watch the breath as you sit in the silent place of meditation. The breath, flowing gently in and out, will soothe the mind and bring you quickly to the place of God. Then you can bring your focus to the *ajna* chakra, the third eye, and visualize your teacher or guru or chosen form of God right there between your eyebrows, seated on a lotus throne with two immaculate white petals.

See the divine form in a golden light. Be still and one-pointed in your concentration. Do not let your mind scatter or run away with thoughts that have no meaning. Instead, be at home in the center of your being and feel the glow of God come over you.

In the depth of meditation, the mind lies still. The mind is like a deep ocean, and in meditation it becomes calm and without waves. As this ocean of consciousness lies still, you can see its clarity, and then your whole being becomes serene. In the serenity of right understanding you will soon be able to master the senses, little by little and then more and more. In meditation no effort is lost. This you must know.

When you emerge from deep meditation, your mind will no longer be scattered and unsettled as it was before. You will feel yourself sustained by the love of God because you will have touched the very essence of divine love with your higher, now purified mind. Feel grateful for any joy in your life, and you will glow with the touch of God. Be content with yourself, and others will be content with you. Be in love with the heart that God has given you, and others will learn from you how to love themselves as God's children.

As a child is born innocent and pure of mind and heart, so are you like a child in your meditation. Follow your mind back to your heart and to that state where you are a special child in the Mother's eyes, in the Mother's heart.

Who Am I?

As a spiritual practice, ask yourself throughout the day, "Who am I? Who am I?" This question will help you to discover the nature of your true Self. As you grope through the fog of ego to find your own image, you become conscious that you are made in the image of God. You will gain the confidence to overcome any defects you think you have, and when meditation grows deep enough, you will be able to receive the glorious view of universal consciousness.

As you meditate on the heart, remember that your being is not limited to your body alone. To identify with the body is ignorance. To identify with the mind is also ignorance. To identify with the ego is greater ignorance still.

As you let these go, you learn to identify with the Self, with God. Then you will come face to face with the bliss of freedom, and your inner life will be transformed. You are not this body, not the senses, not the mind. Feel your whole being merge with the God beyond all limits. The true you is universal and all-pervading, free as the wind and all-knowing. All the realms of knowledge are within you and can be tapped through meditation.

Even after a short time the results will begin to show. Being conscious that you are becoming a mystic—a knower of God and Self—will give you an insight that you never had before. As you begin to identify with the Self or God, you begin to let the rest go. There is wisdom in letting go, and you are wise—much wiser than you think. It is only the ego that tries to make you think that you do not know too much. Meditation undoes the feeling of duality, the feeling of separation, the cause of stress.

You are one with the One. We are all one in the One. We are one with all things of heaven and earth. Use your moments of meditation to understand fully that you are one with the Mother in all her many forms. Feel her shakti and know you have the wisdom to live each day fully in the light of her holiness.

Ask yourself every day, "Who am I?" The nature of every human being is holy. Through meditation, which means your intimate relationship with God, you leave shallowness behind. You begin to form a habit of kindness and compassion. Once you know that God is your innermost source of strength, then you recognize that her divine love is ever present—always there for you to receive and to give to others. There is greatness in you, because there is God in you. And meditation is all about touching upon this greatness of who you really are.

The false ego is born of ignorance and is ever ready to take you off guard. Just when you think you are in your God-heart, you slip back into ego-awareness, and then your mind keeps you from being happy and fulfilled.

The ego always wants something. When you find that your mind is wandering simply say, "Thank you, thank you, thank you." Repeat this like a mantra, be reminded of what you have to be thankful for, and drive away the ego's worthless desires.

Or let your ego melt in the fire of Mother Kali's love. The Mother will let you see the ego for what it is, and you will be willing to give it up in a split second. If you just remember to ask the Mother to take your grief and worry and if you abide in the deepest part of your heart, then the wayward ego has neither place nor voice. The pressure of love is too great for the ego to resist.

The darkness of ego cannot live long on a spiritual path. When you overcome anger and jealousy, the ego begins to burn away on its own funeral pyre. Then there is light and more light. The ego is dark like coal; God is luminous like ten thousand suns. The ego is small and miserable; God the Mother is without beginning or end; she is joy itself. She is unconditional love in its purest form.

Take possession this day of your own life, and never let the ego have its way. The ego has no place in your life, now or ever.

Mindfulness

All your life you have taken certain things for granted. When you learn to be mindful, you will begin to see those things in a new and beautiful light. When you learn to become mindful of everything in your life, everything seems to change: your physical world, your body, your emotional world, your mental world, your spiritual world, and your ability to smile. Look at colors and see how bright they can be. Taste the world. Experience yourself. Taste God this very day.

Meditation will lead you to mindfulness. As you sit in meditation, begin as you usually do. Watch your breath coming in and going out. Now feel this experience of the breath with your heart and not with your mind. Whenever your attention begins to stray, bring the breath back to your heart.

At first it is normal for the attention to stray. Do not let this concern you. Never judge yourself or your meditation. As you learn not to react within, you will learn not to react without.

As you come out of meditation, say to yourself, "Today I will not react at all." Make this a part of your mindfulness. If the element of anger comes at you at any time during the day, remember those words, "I will not react." They will stay in your heart, until needed, for you to use.

That is one example of the practice. As you live with mindfulness, you will be able to tell the difference between when you are attached and when you are detached, when you allow things to bother you and when you do not. All of this is revealed through the attention you give to your thoughts, feelings, and actions when you practice mindfulness. As your awareness grows, it will bring increasing balance to your life.

Set an inner clock for every hour, and on the hour ask yourself if you are paying attention. Remember that mindfulness is the great jewel of the heart. A jewel is precious, and this one is very precious because it brings freedom. When you, the seeker, begin to tell the difference between reacting and mindfulness, then you will begin to understand the law of karma, and when that happens you will become the maker of your own destiny.

Mindfulness is a special clarity of mind. It comes from the wisdom handed down from teacher to student, but you must make it your own through spiritual practice.

Raising Your Awareness

There is a vital force of consciousness in everyone that longs to be fully awakened and put to good use in this lifetime. This power is known as Kundalini Shakti. She is the form of the Mother Goddess who dwells at the base of the spine, coiled three and a half times around the Shiva linga like a serpent in a state of slumber. If she does not awaken, her sleep binds the person to a life of darkness, because her slumber is the ordinary consciousness of the spiritually unawakened person. Kundalini Shakti wants to awaken, and when she does, you become aware of her rising along the sushumna, the central channel of the spine. This rising is her sacred journey to the top of the head, where she merges with Lord Shiva.

This rising of Kundalini Shakti is also your spiritual journey, and along the way, with every one of the chakras (energy centers) she touches and opens like a lotus flower in full bloom, you rise to a higher level of awareness. When you live more and more in the spiritual world, you are drawn ever nearer to God the Mother and God the Father—Shakti and Shiva—in new and wonderful ways. Each day is an adventure.

With the awakening of Kundalini, your *prana*, or life-breath, is carried upward from one chakra to the next, and your desire for God becomes more apparent to yourself and to others. Nourish your mind with thoughts of goodness and service, and then give up thoughts all together. Simply let all thoughts float away as you rise higher and higher in the cloudless sky of divine consciousness.

There is nothing impossible for the soul to accomplish and for the yogi to experience, once this fountain of infinite strength is tapped. By meditating regularly you awaken this latent strength, for Kundalini shows herself through meditation and brings the inner strength of the soul to the forefront.

The true birthright of all human beings is to have Kundalini awaken, to have consciousness rise and reveal its full beauty. As long as Kundalini lies dormant, people cannot use their total capacities. Not even aware of them, most people go through life expressing only a tiny fraction of their shakti. The yogi who learns how to arouse this spiritual energy in meditation experiences Kundalini with great joy under the guidance of a guru or spiritual teacher.

In the morning, meditate on the light of the rising sun. Your consciousness, your inner light, will rise above the body and embrace all the God-qualities. The spiritual energy will rise above the body and direct you to right action. As the Kundalini Shakti rises through the channel in the middle of the spine, she pierces all the chakras, the centers of spiritual energy, one by one. Each one, at her touch, is said to open like a lotus in bloom.

The guru will teach you to meditate on the shining light of wisdom in the fourth chakra in the heart and then to follow the energy upward to the fifth chakra in the throat and then up to the sixth chakra, the third eye between the eyebrows. You will learn to meditate on the third eye and visualize the brilliant light of God there between the eyebrows. From there, the Kundalini Shakti rises to the thousand-petaled lotus at the top of the head and merges in ecstasy with Lord Shiva. Then united, Shakti and Shiva rise as one out of this seventh chakra to the eighth chakra above the head.

As your awareness rises, you begin to come in touch with your higher Self. There is a light, filled with love, that shines from your higher Self and sees deeper and farther than the human eye.

Practicing meditation in your quiet moments leads to your fuller awareness. Then you will want to practice this mindfulness throughout the day. Breathing deep into the heart will bring you patience. Through watching the breath, the *prana*, you will become more and more understanding toward yourself and others. When you learn to listen to this breath, you will follow your divine instincts. The great power of Kundalini can be heard like a sweet voice when you are in the moment, and you begin to experience your true Self.

Sometimes the experience is intense and sometimes it is subtle. In any case, always be aware of your own heart, and you will naturally become aware that you can take care of others with inexhaustible love. As Kundalini awakens, you will feel yourself become the boundless expansion of divine love. You will discover so much love in your heart that you will have no choice but to share it with all whom you meet.

Love that is true is never divided and never subjected to differences. Love is interfaith in its purest form. We are all One, all equal, even in our seeming differences. Love knows only one reality, and that reality is that we are all One.

The Breath and Its Power

Do you know that you carry within you a powerful force that you can put to use at all times and in all places? That force is prana. Prana is the breath flowing in and flowing out. Prana is the life-force, and beyond that, prana is deathless and all-pervading.

Prana has many forms. Part of the spiritual journey is to learn to have mastery over the prana in all its forms. Breath practices to master prana are called pranayama. Lord Vayu, the ancient god of the wind, is the king of pranayama and of all the different pranas that bring life to the body and mind.

The prana is to the yogi what electricity is to a light bulb. It is light and life. A true yogi is one who has control over the prana, has mastery over every part of life. This mastery is gained by watching the breath.

Through the breath you cultivate bhakti, devotion to God, and you become a bhakta, a devotee. By watching the breath, you can activate the heart. The heart needs to pump love, and when it does, the bhakta hidden in you emerges. It is as simple as this.

As you begin to feel the heartstrings stir with love, the breath becomes deeper of its own accord and replaces the ego-breath, which is short and not deep at all. The ego-breath remains only on the surface of life and death. In contrast, the vital energy of the devotee's breath allows you to experience the full course of a life filled with love. The ego begins and ends with the lower mind. The bhakta's experience begins and ends with love.

We live in two worlds, one of the body and mind, one of the spirit. Watching the breath with great awareness, you are brought into a space that is not accessible to the ordinary, unawakened mind. In the wakeful state of the higher mind, everything changes. In the ordinary state your thoughts are ruled by the ego. In the subtle state of divine thought, it is not the ego that rules but the purified heart. Beyond that lies the even subtler state of Kali-consciousness or God-consciousness, and that is the great consciousness of liberation.

When you focus on the breath, you do not allow yourself to think you are held back by the demands or the limitations of the body or the mind. Your body is the one that you received owing to your karma, and so is your mind, with all its habits and tendencies. The breath will remind you that the body and the mind that you think bind you to this world are in fact the tools that will free you from the wheel of life and death. Breathe in this awareness, and be grateful for your life on earth. As you follow your spiritual path, be grateful for these tools you have been given, and be especially grateful for the breath, which is most powerful of all.

The Spiritual Heart

When you ask how to get closer to God, the answer is inside of you. All the answers to questions not even asked are inside of you.

After being on the spiritual path for a while, there comes a time when you make up your mind that *this is it*, and you go ahead with determination. You know that in your heart and soul there is a memory that you must trust, and that memory is your love for God that will guide you. When you learn to maintain the right balance, all you have to do is sit quietly and listen to your heart.

We have all come from the womb of the great Mother. This womb is always there, open and waiting for us to return to it in meditation.

At any time we can return to the source. This is the ever-present possibility in everyone's life, regardless of one's religion, creed, color, gender, sexual orientation, or any other God-given uniqueness. The secret is to learn how to be yourself in the joy of God.

When there was yet no sound pervading the creation, the vibration of love gave birth to the sound of the universal heartbeat. As you become experienced in yogic breathing, your individual soul becomes more attuned to the universal, supreme Self. As you listen to your heart during meditation, imagine that your heart-sounds are the sounds and rhythms of Kali's drumbeat. You do not need to imagine, because they are. Kali is always dancing across your heart, even as her beautiful black feet are always dancing on the snow-white breast of the reclining Lord Shiva.

Now breathe in the living essence of Lord Shiva at the center of your being. This essence is light.

Listen now to the sound of Shiva's sacred drum of creation, pulsating within the cave of the heart, where the soul dwells in the warm glow of love. Breathe into the heart as deeply as you can and hold the breath, bringing your awareness to the heart's expansion.

Now as if your breath had wings, send out this breath of love all over the world. Let it radiate from you.

Next, feel that love flow upward, touching every spiritual center within you. It rises from chakra to chakra, and each new state of awareness prepares you for the next higher state. When the spiritual energy known as Kundalini rises from the third chakra, the power center in the abdomen, and reaches into the fourth or heart chakra, the state that you experience is the great opening of the heart.

One person has the power to change something on earth by just being aware. Awareness is the key. After breathing deeply in and out, as your breath comes back to normal, ask the Mother to bring you deeper than ever before into your heart. Feel as if you are journeying into a space of grace that you never tasted before. Listen to your heartbeat and go into it, deep into bliss. Hear the word *anahata*, with the accent on the second syllable. Anahata is the unstruck sound, the OM from before there was sound, the vibration of divine bliss. This is the heart chakra. Feel a tenderness for your own heart. Feel a tenderness for the hearts of others.

To bring your awareness to the heart chakra is to expand your ability to love and serve. You only have to breathe the love of your own God, of your own path, deeply into this space in the middle of your chest. Feel the warmth spread throughout your body, and then breathe out. Fix your attention on the lotus of the heart. As you center your awareness there, a light will shine from the heart. This light will lead you to the practice of mindfulness in all your day's doings.

When you are fully drenched in such concentration, you cannot be hurt by the insensitivity of others, nor can you be insensitive to them. Self-doubt and unworthiness loosen their grasp on a heart opened by love. Your full awareness will be centered in love, and what you feel in the heart becomes a state of harmony that spreads and spreads.

It is all a matter of being aware of who you are and of your relationship to God and to others. When you discover the supreme devotion you are capable of, the power of love that you possess will let you know in the depths of your being how much you are loved and how much you can love.

When you learn to move and act with the freedom of love, your karma becomes good and knowledge glows in the heart. In this knowledge that is free of doubt, the existence of the permanent Self need never prove itself, for you know beyond all doubt the permanent reality of the Self that shines like a million suns. In its light the unreal has no shine to it any more.

Therefore, let all sense of ego vanish as you understand that there is nothing outside yourself that you need or need to find out or to know. Nothing exists outside of the Mother; nothing exists without her. When your heart is opened in devotion and you become a bhakta, a devotee of God, you hold this immense ocean of wisdom within you.

Prayer

Life is not always pleasant, and often things do not go the way we would like them to. When you pray, ask for strength to conquer all miseries in life. You will soon begin to learn the God-strength that is in you, and you may be surprised that you are able to confront any condition that comes your way. There is no tribulation in life that you cannot handle, so never be ungenerous with prayer. There is no need to confine your prayer to a few words. God is always available to all people, ever willing to hear their prayers.

You may ask, "How do I pray?" In praying, you only need to surrender to your own inner divinity and feel the expansion of this sacredness toward the universal Self. Soar into the heavens with prayer and worship, and feel that you are having the experience of divine communion. When your heart expands by regular sessions of prayer, you begin to recognize your true nature of love. Let your heart bloom as you pray for others. Pray for love for everyone. Pray for world peace. There is nothing impossible for the one who prays.

As you pray for others, whatever their background, ethnicity, sexual orientation, religion, or spiritual path, vibrations of the Mother's divine energy will come to you as you give up the dark thoughts of judgment. Nourish your heart with the diversity of all, and make your prayer universal.

When you pray, the feeling is so much more important than the words you use. When you feel the heart open, the words of prayer and devotion will flow naturally from the heart. Let the breath open your being like a lotus blossom.

When you get into the habit of prayer, you will feel yourself expand in love. Surrender to the Divine within you now, and feel the wonder and the joy of that simple act of surrender. This will open your heart to the greatness of God. When you worship God in any of her many forms, you are letting her bring you to the Formless where all religions are the same and God is available to everyone.

When prayer seeps into your moment—any moment—then that moment becomes sacred. Pray whenever you have time, and if you do not have time, then make the time to feel this oneness with the universal form of God, the Formless.

The Simple Act of Letting Go

You may sometimes get a little confused by the different teachings about surrendering to God or making an effort of your own. Really, it is not so difficult at all: you simply surrender to the great God within your own being. When you truly surrender your individual will (the one that causes a lot of trouble) to the divine will, you will find that you have in you all that you need to succeed. You do not need to think any more about what *you* need to do. There is great beauty in this, because when you can say, "I surrender, my God, to your will" and really mean it, that is not a giving up of anything, but a freeing. It is you freeing yourself from all doubt and confusion, and that is refreshing and magical.

The teacher or guru lives to bring you to the will of God, to the pure joy of service and compassion that is God's will. The bhakta knows of this divine joy. Every morning I ask my guru, "What do you want me to do this day to serve you and humanity?" Because I have surrendered my own will, the answer is always there. "Live your life feeding everyone" is the answer.

I enjoy spreading this great teaching on service to all of you, because this is one way that you can advance toward your higher

Self. There is nothing greater in the guru's life than to bring the seeker toward Self-knowledge, the awareness of his or her own deepest, widest, and highest being. That is why when you allow the lower self to yield and let yourself be ruled by the higher Self within the silent cave of your heart, the guru watches with a heart full of bliss.

We call this silent space "the cave of the heart." This inner space is at the heart of all religions and beliefs. In any religion or path the teacher guides you there to find the real side of you. If you are devoted to the Mother Kali, for example, then God in the form of Kali will work through you to serve others. This moment I am thinking of our Kali of the cremation ground and the joy she brings when we can let go of all that we do not need and she can reduce it to ash.

Yet, there are so many other divine forms and so many other religions. Think of your God and breathe in deeply this moment the will of universal consciousness. Hold the breath and feel the joy of this connection spread throughout your whole body. On the interfaith path, you only need to be open and joyful—even to that which is different and unique. In every tradition spiritually minded people are drawn together through the love of God, and teacher or guru. It is that love that allows them to let go of all that is petty and small. Look now into your hearts and feel the sweetness of surrendering to God within your heart.

Love Unites

Spiritual teaching is like nectar, to be received as *prasad*, or divine grace. It comes straight from the love in the guru's heart. This is no ordinary love, for it is lit by the great light of consciousness. A phrase or even one word from the guru can ignite that same light in every one of you.

Worldly nature is not the true you; it is only a slight shadow of your divine Self. My prayer has always been that all my children attain God-consciousness and the ability to see beyond duality. This can be activated through meditating on the breath of love. Doing this, you can get rid of all forces of darkness and division and come into the great light of your God-heart. Make God the center of your life this day and every day and watch your worldly nature fade away.

Ask Maya, the creator of illusion, to take her leave and the Mother Kali to bring you reality in the form of love. The principle of cosmic reality in all religions is love. Love is pure consciousness, and in unconditional love there is no duality, only the oneness of lover and beloved. Allow your mind to enjoy the sweetness of loving God.

Realize everyone as part of God, not as apart from God. Realize the world as the Self, and become this day who you truly are—the universal Self in full bloom. Then your smile can surge through any turbulent ocean and shine through the brilliance of the sun itself.

Why not smile and make someone happy? Feel divine this day, and through every action promote peace and harmony in the world. Walk tall, feeling the gracious hand of God upon you, and allow her divine will to be done.

The Word, Spoken and Unspoken

The abundance of the universe is yours. You only have to ask God to awaken you to that understanding, and everything you need for the spiritual path will be provided. Whenever you have thoughts of God and are about to speak out loud or pray silently to God or Goddess, a divine energy comes into the fifth chakra, located at the level of the throat.

This energy, or shakti, lives between the spoken and unspoken words, and its power is immense. Try to become aware that as you utter words, there is an energy that rises through the spine and enters first into the heart, then passes up to the throat and rides out into the world on the prana, the outgoing breath.

When there are dark thoughts of passion and power, of greed and anger, the energy coming from the lower chakras goes right around the heart and remains untouched by love. When it passes out through the throat as unkind or violent or harmful speech, it is still clouded by a terrible darkness. Because the power of the word is so immense, this darkness lingers and enters back into you through the incoming breath. When you do harm to others, you do harm to yourself also.

As you speak to your chosen form of God or Goddess, either silently or out loud, the vibrations of that speech are vibrations of light. They bring you the capacity to love that spreads throughout you to all the chakras. This prayer is a form of divine communication that transforms you inwardly. In the same way, when you direct your communication with God or Goddess through an image in a shrine or temple, the power of divine speech brings life to the image. Everywhere in the world where sacred images are bowed down to, prayed to, and revered, these places are alive with the divine presence.

Sit quietly with your heart's chosen God or Goddess, your true beloved, and feel how easy it is to attain communion with the Deity. Any divine form has the capacity to awaken your heart to love and joy, and when you feel awakened, you find yourself filled with good will and kindness for everyone.

With this divine communion—this sense of "oneness with"—you will find yourself surrendering more and more to God or Goddess within, and with the joy of love will come a sense of commitment. As the mind becomes increasingly pure, the heart moves to become increasingly active in serving others. This motion of the heart is not like your ordinary, limited feelings; instead, it reflects a communication with the universal Self.

To feel instant joy in your life, all you need to do is to use the power of the word to be connected to the Divine. Just say a holy name over and over again. Do this for five minutes at a time and then sit quietly and feel God or Goddess come to you. Where did this teaching come from? It rose up through the divine energy of the Mother Vak, who is the goddess of the creative word. Through our spiritual teachers it became the words that guide us.

Know that the power of the word is immense, because that power, that shakti that speaks to us and teaches us, is the Divine Mother herself.

The Company You Keep

It is easier to be open to God-consciousness when you have the company of other spiritual seekers. Holy company is called *satsang.* To be in an environment in which you can grow more and more each day is a reward of your good karma. The mysteries of the heart unfold more readily as you live with those who love God and Goddess and love itself. Satsang gives mutual support to everyone involved. It helps to bring about understanding of the joys of meditation.

In satsang, an aspirant after God has many others with whom to share the experiences of life. Shakti flows from one person to another in the company of God. The heart holds the greatest amount of shakti, and this shakti always flows when there are many with the same, yet also unique, ideas. A true spiritual community is always fresh and filled with life, no matter how long it has been together.

In satsang you learn to read your own heart clearly. You all have the ability to overcome the defects that you think you have. Do not let the mind master you, but let the heart reveal the boundless joy that abides within you. Watch your companions' lives and develop patience, endurance, and persistence from their example. When you see those qualities in the lives of those around you, you will understand your own impatience with yourself. You will learn to endure and to persist in whatever you must do.

With the support of satsang, you can more easily begin to overcome different fears in yourself, and when you conquer those fears, you are ever more free to pursue the joy of God. A life in God is a life filled with adventures of the Mother and service of humanity. A life in God brings you to understand that you are the eternal Self, and to live with the eternal Self revealed is the greatest freedom there is.

Yes, You Can!

Do not sell yourself short on any of your abilities. Look inside and see if it is time to expand and extend yourself toward God, if it is time to go beyond your habits. When you make a mistake, isn't it so much easier to admit it and start afresh than to keep on defending your old habits?

When you keep compounding your mistakes by defending everything you do, you are learning nothing and creating deeper and deeper mental ruts. These are called *samskaras*, and they bind you like chains.

When you do not extend yourself to your true spiritual length and you pull back from any chance to grow, then you remain small in your efforts and small of heart. Do not let the heart shrivel and dry up. You have a beautiful heart; keep it open and beating with the joy of God.

As you become more aware of your God-filled heart expanding, expanding, expanding, you find that you have more compassion for others as well as for yourself. There is a great creative power, shakti, within you. Where and how can you use the power of shakti to do the most good for yourself and humanity?

There is so much more to you than you realize. You are the total of everything you were in every lifetime. You can use this experience of many lifetimes now, even though your mind does not remember.

Your guru offers you every opportunity to know who you are, to expand as fast as you can, and to achieve happiness for yourself and others. Your guru can arouse your spiritual energy, Kundalini, to rise and manifest in your life. You become stronger and stronger as Mother Kundalini awakens and starts her journey up the spine, touching each chakra along the way and stimulating the petals to open fully and bring you spiritual bliss. She rises to the thousand-petaled lotus at the crown of the head and merges in bliss with Lord Shiva. Follow her there and then way over the top of the head to the purest place of your God-Self.

Then purify your heart with the heat of divine passion. You will be surprised at what happens. Anger, lust, greed, and jealousy have no place in your life any more. Fears can be banished by meditating on the courage that is yours in the thousand-petaled lotus, the crown chakra.

Everyone has this God-courage; everyone is a gigantic vessel of truth and wisdom. Go into that place of silent wisdom, and then work to bring peace and joy to the world. Everyone is a part of this work, and there is much to be done.

All day long just say to God, "I love you, God." Very simply say, "I love you, God." Lose yourself in God this day. That's all it takes. You can do this even as you live your life. Yes, you can! All day long just call on God. I promise that God will hear your silent words.

The Art of Listening

A big part of spiritual practice is quieting the mind, and there is a way to do this that you may have not thought about before. It's called listening. Nothing more, just listening.

As long as there are words, it is good to hear the words of others, for this act of listening, by focusing the mind, quiets the mind. Also, by listening to others, you give them strength, and while you give them your strength, so much more is coming to you. When you allow others to hear their own voices, you create good karma with your stillness.

There is beauty in listening to someone with an open heart, and as you listen to another, you learn to hear yourself better, too. When you let the other person be free in his or her words, you can see how much compassion you have in your heart.

You may be surprised. It does not matter what your religion is or who your teacher is: as you come closer and closer to the heart of the teaching, you begin to listen more closely and more deeply to others. All the thoughts of your mind leave as you are hearing them speak, for you are beginning to listen with the heart. As you give yourself over to other people's hearts, you become whole within yourself.

Even as God the Mother is interested always in you, be interested in the well-being of others. Be always in the moment when someone else speaks, and do not forget to give your heart. The moment you think of someone who needs your love, send that love freely, no matter what.

Your body is visible to everyone. Your spirit must be felt, too. It is the same for the person who comes to you, needing to be heard. You can easily see this person; now it is time for you to recognize the spirit within. When you can see someone else's beauty, you are better able to see your own.

Do you know your own beauty? Listening to others as well as to your inner self will open your eyes, and all judgment will melt away in your heart of love. The essence of love, which is your own God-essence, will teach you to live in the spirit of non-judgment. As you learn not to judge others, you learn also not to judge yourself so harshly. Remember, prejudice in any form makes the wise ignorant, and acceptance makes the ignorant wise.

If you can truly hear when others speak, surely you will hear when the Mother speaks to you. Of this have no doubt. When you have finished listening to someone else, sit quietly and listen to you. What are your dreams and your desires? Listen with all your heart to what you have to say. Be very still and hear the words of your soul. The atmosphere around you will be filled with a joyous vibration. You will feel your heart expand and unfold with a huge amount of love. Feel this as an inner act of worship, and offer flowers with your mind's eye to your own inner light. Not only you, but everyone else will benefit from this moment.

A Bouquet of Offerings

In a world overrun by wars and grief and pain, it is good to make time to think of the beauty of God the Mother and God the Father. It is good to pause for a moment of worship, to offer your fear and insecurity to the God of your choice, the God of your heart, in this very moment.

By thinking in this way, you can lessen your fears. It takes a person of real faith to step out of the norm of everyday living and say, "I am willing to try to change the world with my love. Mother, just show me how." Let that be your intent. The Mother will show you how to make a difference.

Each human being is responsible for his or her actions, and it is by your actions that other people can learn of love. With every act of kindness you are already changing the earth in a small way. Every small moment of love counts.

Do not look for outlets of instant gratification. Instead, shatter the empty desires of your active mind by meditating on the Mother's loving heart. Find it in yourself to seek the Mother's hand. Be hungry for God, and let her consume your ego-mind while your heart is drenched in her love. Ask the Mother to liberate you from wanting what will hurt your spiritual progress.

Make a difference by offering your God a flower today. Yes, that is right: offer a flower. Lord Krishna says in the Bhagavad Gita,

"Whoever offers to me even a leaf, or flower, fruit, or water with devotion, I verily accept that with great delight." Let this flower be a symbol of all that you intend to do and all that you have done. Let yourself think of this as a moment of bringing delight to God. In this way you can stop the restlessness of your own mind and feel a warm feeling seep into your heart.

You cannot do worship without intent, and the highest intent is simply to please God. The greatness of worship and prayer is that you know in your heart that you are being listened to. Call on the Mother before you start your meditation and ask her to guide your words and prayers. The Mother Kali is called the reliever of difficulties. It is she who destroys confusion and burns up all your karma. Let your own heart be the *dhuni* (fire pit) in which the Mother's sacred fire burns.

As meditation becomes an indispensable part of your daily life, you will find more and more peace in your being. As your mind grows still, waves of bliss can be yours. You will find that your mind is not so difficult to control once you get into the habit of being in your heart. As your meditation deepens, the active mind becomes the God-mind. When unwanted thoughts come, you no longer let them upset you. Instead, you let them merely pass by, and you smile to yourself until they are gone.

When the unwanted thoughts go from the mind, some small measure of grief and pain goes from this world. This, which is so pleasing to God, begins with the intent of your heart.

Choosing to Heal

You will always have choices to make. What will you choose today? Choose to be happy as soon as you start your day. Raise your hands over your head, and with head thrown back thank God for a new and wonderful dawn. And know that when you are happy and content, it is not just for yourself.

Everyone has the power to heal; yet the only healer is the power of God. When you tune into this power and your heart is filled with love, other people's hearts are healed just by being around you. As you become established in higher God-consciousness, the healing power spreads out, and all can feel the warmth of its rays. Can you even begin to know how much warmth and love and strength you have in you? Do you know how radiant you become when you care for others?

As you meditate, your mind begins to vibrate with waves of light and kindness. You first become kind to yourself, and then the generosity of love spills out to others. When you send out prayers for the healing of others, truly you are healed yourself.

For a moment let's consider the alternative. When you are angry and seek revenge, when you turn on others, your mind becomes crippled, and your heart grows brittle. Do you want to be in the sunlight of caring or in the darkness of selfishness?

Watch your actions when you care for others. Watch how your tears change to laughter, and watch how your laughter changes the tears of others to laughter and smiles. You have the power to make great and wonderful choices. You have the power to have a positive influence. Bring joy to someone else, and learn about your healing powers.

To Forgive Is Divine

Forgiveness is like a sparkling gem, because it has many facets that reflect its beauty.

Sometimes a little forgiveness of yourself brings on a whole lot of compassion for others. Leave all your feelings of failure behind, and come into the light of divine love.

You need not run from past mistakes, you need not run to them, and you need not be run by them. You only need to learn from yesterday so you can live today more fully. Stand up strong and courageous—in your name and in the name of your God—and forgive yourself for anything that needs forgiving.

When you can forgive yourself, you are able to forgive others. If everyone in the world came into the healing light of forgiveness, then all hate would abate and love would rule. Every religion teaches forgiveness and shines with its light. There is no need, ever, for anyone to linger in the darkness.

Forgiveness belongs to the shining treasure of love deep in the cave of your heart. It will bring much happiness to your life. Breathe in and let your attention rest in the lotus of your heart as you hold the breath. Then breathe out the sanctified breath to all the world. Share your love with everyone, and the world will become a better place.

The more you breathe in this way, the less you will be attached to things of the world. Your faults will begin to disappear. As you are more in touch with the treasure of forgiveness in your heart, vow never again to be cruel towards anyone. If you are not yet able to admire another's good qualities, then simply walk away until you can find something in another's heart that is good.

When you learn to be kind to others and kind to yourself, you will recognize that kindness is the path of all great sages. Kindness is universal to all spirituality. As long as you live in the power of kindness you are sure to hear the inner voice of God. You can feel God's heartbeats in your own heart, the divine presence in your blood, and God's sacred breath in your own breath. Then there is nothing to stop you from making each day a day filled with kindness and compassion.

Through forgiveness of yourself and others, you become a child of love and joy and peace. Feel the peace of forgiveness in your heart, and send its healing power out to others all over the world.

With Eyes of Compassion

Mother Tara, who is another form of the Mother, was born from the tears of the Buddha of Compassion. Because she is the personification of the Mother's unconditional love, her eyes shine with the beauty of kindness. At the same time, it is her nature to protect her children at all times, and those who go against her children's goodness must certainly feel her wrath.

If you call on her to rid yourself of any ignorance, she will come to you and take away all signs of ignorance and dullness. She will remove that dark energy that is their cause. When you are freed from all the heaviness that holds you back, you will feel a certain freedom in her compassion.

As you advance on the spiritual path, your sensitivity to yourself becomes greatly enhanced. You become attuned to deeper feelings of God in yourself, and serenity follows. In your own inner quiet, you will feel sensitivity for others as well. You can give yourself a chance to grow by practicing kindness and compassion, and when you are sincere in this, you will find that it comes to you quickly.

Do people feel comfortable coming to you with their problems? Is your heart wide open? If people come to you, then they know that you hold God the Mother in your heart and are able to help. If they come to you in this way, they bring you a gift of grace, for by simply listening and speaking from your heart, you bring peace, understanding, and happiness to their hearts. This simple act of compassion will bring you into a pure state of God-awareness.

Do not forget to listen with your heart as well as your ears. The person who opens up to you out of need wants desperately to escape the pain of a certain situation. Think of how you would like to be spoken to if you were in pain. When you speak from your heart, talk gently, be conscious of your thoughts, *and make sure you are not judging.* Be sure that you never think that you are the doer.

When you live fully in God, your voice becomes the voice of goodness. Keep your breath steady, and breathe deeply into the heart without showing it. Keep your spine straight and offer everything to the Mother. Then when you speak to those in need, you become the Mother. Woman or man, you become the Mother.

When you sit in the silence of your heart and feel the love of the guru flow through you for a few minutes each day, you will become filled with the light of God. Others will see this light. When someone is in despair, go to your own heart and give that person your love. It takes courage to wipe away someone's tears as your own heart is breaking, but when you live your life to the best of your ability, you will understand that all the kindness in the world is already inside of you, just waiting to come out.

With this teaching of compassion in mind, aspire this day to know your own purity of mind, body, and soul. Aspire to serve as never before. Aspire to understand and accept everyone's path, not just your own. Never be satisfied with limited concepts of wisdom, but remember that you have within yourself the wisdom that can awaken you to your God-nature, which is the Self.

Let nothing get in your way. If you are unsure, let the clouds of doubt and despair leave you and feel in their place the presence of God's love. Moments of doubt will come and go. This is only natural, yet the heart knows no doubt when it comes to love. Consciously escort your doubts to the breath and then breathe them all out over the head. You will begin to relax in the joy of loving God. You need only the moment to quiet the mind and ease the soul. To get rid of doubt is to be in perfect serenity.

Let the principle of divine love permeate your life. When you recognize that you have a burning passion for God in your heart, you will know also that without that passion there can be no compassion. Your passion for God will never allow your compassion to dry up. You will always be filled with a deep love for God and humanity.

As you keep this passion and compassion awake by breathing deeply and mindfully, you will constantly renew yourself and your ability to help others. You will have all the strength and the patience you need to serve those in need.

If you make your eyes kind, others can feel this kindness. Do you know how you can make your eyes kind? All you have to do is breathe in love deep into your heart and let that love reach your eyes. Then breathe out this love, and your eyes will tell the tale of your compassionate heart. When you have space in your heart for all, the heart accommodates by growing ever larger.

Let the Mother Tara shine within you this day as you follow the religion of the heart, which is kindness and compassion.

Divine Love

In the Katha Upanishad it is said, "Not he who has not ceased from doing wrong, nor he who knows no peace, no concentration, nor he whose mind is filled with restlessness can grasp God, wise and clever though he may be."

It does not matter how smart you are or how much knowledge you hold in your mind. It only matters how big your heart is and how focused you are on God. Love is the greatest of all teachers, because when the heart is open, then wisdom and knowledge come automatically. The desires of the ego-self melt in the fire of the bhakta's love for God. The bhakta, the devotee of God, destroys karma by loving God so much and so well.

No matter what your religion or your path, become a bhakta. Feel the depth of your love, and feel you are saturated with God's love. One whose devotion to God comes from the heart fixes the mind constantly on thoughts of God the beloved. When one becomes single-minded and the mind is on God at all times, then the heart is open wide and never closes. This path of love is called Bhakti Yoga, and it is devotion in the truest meaning of the word.

It is important that you find yourself in your heart more and more and that you merge with your beloved God in your heart. The force of divine love will heal and inspire and reveal to you that you are very close to God. This unseen force shows you how to grow, because it is always there to guide you. What could ever turn you away from love?

The most intense devotion is called ,. When it begins to pervade your being, you will find that you are a mirror of love. As you come closer to God, you begin to find yourself. You are God's love itself, the spirit of pure goodness. Observe your pure spirit, and experience love like never before. Perceive yourself as love's force, and let it guide your every thought and action. You will see that love is all there is.

There is no illusion in God's or Goddess's love. There is no beginning or end to love. It is like the great river Ganga, always flowing, always knowing, never ending. Always flowing, always knowing, never-ending joy.

On the Path of Love

The path of love is the path of surrender. When you put your life in the hands of God, you begin at once to feel supported. All sorrows that have clung to you and that you have clung to in the past fall off as you lay your head in the lap of the Mother. Realizing the pureness of loving God so fully, you begin to feel God in your life at all times. Then you become aware of the soul's inborn relation to God, flowing twenty-four hours a day.

Saying the name of God as a mantra, over and over, you can feel the inborn seed of God's love being nurtured.

As long as you are stuck in the world and the things of the world, you are in deep slumber. By breathing in deep breaths of love, you can gain insight into what you are afraid of. When you relax in the knowledge that you are in love with the Divine, you can alleviate anxiety, depression, and even phobias. If you can imagine a loving father and a caring mother always holding you, think how much better your life will be.

Stress and anxiety take their toll by bringing you to a place of unworthiness, and when your self-esteem diminishes, it is hard to have a true love for God. Do not fool yourself that you are unworthy of loving God or unworthy of being loved. Become aware of the love that lies deep in the soul and begin to wake from the slumber of the world.

At first the bhakta's union with God is so very intimate that the devotee keeps it protected in the privacy of the heart. Only after a while the bhakta cannot hold it in the heart any more. It must be shared.

God-love is both the love of God and the love for God. This same God-love pours out for all human beings. When you put aside every difference—all duality—and feel the Oneness, then your heart shines like the sun. You understand that we are all human beings and we all wish for a better world for everyone. These wishes must first come true in our hearts before they can come true in the world. When our hearts are at peace, this peace can be felt all over the earth.

Practice devotion all this day, trying not to have one dry moment. Be ever filled with the juice of the Mother. Wake up from the slumber of unknowing and see everything around you with new eyes. Dig into your heart and unfold a newness that has always been.

As you discover more and more love inside of you, it will be like a spring of magical waters, as sacred as the water of the Ganga. Let this current of love flow all through you, all around you, and toward everyone else with whom you come into contact.

This current is a river of light. Yes, there is light within and throughout your being. Close your eyes and see this light between your brows, a shining orb of love ready to lift you to your universal Mother.

Now is the time to feel the grace. Be steady in your devotion and feel God in every moment of your life. If there are times when you feel yourself drifting away from this sacred space of inner stillness, ask the Mother to draw you back, to open your heart again. Learn to pick the ripened fruit of love, and throughout each day maintain a deep serenity. You will understand that this space of grace in the moment is both calming and energizing, because God is both profound peace and all-powerful shakti.

Whether the divine form is Jewish, Christian, Buddhist, Hindu, or belonging to any other religion, it does not matter. To love one's teacher or guru is also to practice bhakti, because what one truly loves in the teacher is God. There comes into human consciousness the understanding that the love for guru and God are the same love, and this divine love, this bhakti, surpasses all other love. The beauty of any form of God or Goddess or guru will eventually take you into the formless One, which is your own state of God-being. When you rise above the chaos of the world, you enter into a state of spiritual awareness where you live your life as one with God. This is the goal on the path of devotion.

The Moment Is Holiness

Can you feel the love of God all around you? When you are still, you can feel as if you are holding hands with the Mother and know in the depth of your heart that you are never alone. This sharing of yourself with God is a connection that you have always had, whether you are aware of it or not. It is your own beauty, but how often have the events of your day made you forget this beauty that is truly your own? God's love is present whenever you are able to be still and to let go. She, the Mother, is always in the present, and you are the one that God the Mother loves to love. This love is timeless, yet it lives in the moment. That is why when you live out of the moment, you feel more pain than joy.

Life is sacred, and you learn about this sacredness when you live in the now. In what ways can you find your holiness and the holiness of others? You can look into your own heart for forgiveness, and soon you will be forgiving others. Or you can take the name of God and sing it to yourself all this day. Take the name of the Goddess and sing it to yourself all this day. When you do so, others will see a brightness in you and will be drawn to you with love and affection. Your heart lotus will unfold and your capacity to feel, truly to feel, will grow.

In the moment you find that you are the truth of love, and through this love your purpose in life is revealed. How far do you think that God the Mother would let you stray as long as you keep the moment alive with the passionate fire of love? You are the reality of God, and God is your reality.

Through loving God and Goddess in any form, your life becomes sacred. When God becomes accessible, you create a circle of calmness all around you. You are kind to all who come to you, gracious to yourself and others. In the love of each person, you will feel the love of God and Goddess.

And never think that this loving is what you need to be doing—just do it. Just do it, and feel the way it feels. Just feel. Just be.

In this state you will always have reverence for life. With that sense of reverence, you will be drawn every day in the early dawn to ask God to lead you to where the stillness of love is. As the mind becomes more still, there comes to the human heart the joy of being in the silent moment of God. This is the transformation that comes to one in love with the sacredness of life.

Seek out the Mother's love and live in her arms every day.

Approach the holy gate of reality by understanding your own God-beauty. You cannot fail to see this beauty as you sit in the stillness of God's moment each day; soon you will begin to look forward to this stillness. You do not lose the world in meditation. Instead the world becomes embraced by the love within your soul and by the ability you have to serve others.

It is a matter of putting love into action. The path of service starts with gratefulness. Think to yourself, *I am sustained by the love of God; I function in this love of God; I am the love of God.* To say these words will ease your heart and soul.

When there is love in your heart, you care for others, and this caring becomes your strength. Living in the moment and being in love with your guru, your guru's guru, God the Mother, and God the Father dissolves all illusions of time and space. If you are sincere in your love, illusion cannot grasp you.

Know that God is unchanging and will always be unchanged. No matter how the world changes around you, God, who is holiness, stays the same. There is holiness in the moment, the holiness of eternity. When you are in the moment, you are in eternity; you are of God and God is of you. God offers her love to you freely as a flame of devotion that is yours to cherish in the depth of your being, a sacred flame that can never be put out. Each moment that you pay attention, your life will become fresh and new. Do not deprive yourself of one moment of the Mother's gentle caress.

Connecting

When you find yourself living in lower worlds, you find yourself living in loneliness. When you find yourself mired in negativity, you feel cut off from all sense of goodness and from all sense of joy. In times like that, look up and feel the constant love that the Mother has for you. She is always giving and gives equally to all. In the midst of a world gone mad with wars and pain, she is always there in your heart. You can remind yourself by repeating her name, over and over.

As you repeat any name of God or Goddess, the heart becomes filled with that presence. You begin to notice that your life flows more smoothly. As you constantly say the name of God, that which caused you so much pain will be consumed. Laziness, lethargy, and insensitivity will be reduced. Depression and restlessness will go as the heaviness of negativity finds no place in the heart filled with love. That love will take you out of your loneliness.

There in the heart, the Mother in all her forms is with you twenty-four hours a day. She watches over you always, even when you forget that her eyes are on you, and she will guide you back to your heart if you simply call out her name. They who dig deep find the wisdom that exists in the heart from the beginning of time. All who love God with every part of their being speak from this inner light.

No one is equal to one who loves both God and humanity. When you make another person sad, then your own God-heart will be sad. To bring joy to others is to open yourself to joy. Therefore, make sure you treat people in a way that they always have love and dignity. This becomes natural when you follow the interfaith path of acceptance.

A spiritual experience springs from the depth of the heart. Communication with God becomes like a flowing river, never stopping, always moving, touching everything and everyone. In this flowing river, the higher wisdom is set free in the seeker's heart, and then a deeper understanding of the relationship with God develops.

I long to reveal this bhakti moment, this surging of devotion, and to teach you how to swim in the current of the Mother's love. Live in the spirit of prema, the intensely intimate love of God that brings one to bliss. Whoever reaches the God that lives deep within the heart of love knows that *love* is another word for God.

The Interfaith Path

The teachings that you receive from the guru are the teachings passed from guru to disciple since ancient times and also the wisdom pointed out to you that you already possess deep within your own being. You love God in the depth of your heart, but there are times when you forget that. Sometimes life's circumstances bring other thoughts to your mind. But if you always think of God first and foremost, all else will fall into place.

As you begin to seek, you first hold tight to the guru's feet. Then you feel your ignorance, your pride, and your prejudice begin to dissolve away. In the end, goodness always prevails, no matter how long it takes.

God's grace-giving power fills the devotee's heart and keeps it filled whenever the devotee breathes in with awareness of God. The breath allows you to know beyond doubt that where there is God there is love in a full and fragrant form. As you love God more and more, you can form a circle of love that extends outside of your being, expanding more and more. Others can feel it, and then they want the same for themselves. You see, loving God is contagious.

The God that you love has many names and many forms, and they are all one. Those who follow the interfaith path understand this and love all the forms of God and all those who worship God in any form. The interfaith path accepts every religion and way of life.

But when you are ignorant of all that God is, you think that God is different from love, and then fear takes hold of the mind. God and love are truly the same. Just remember that God is within reach of everyone on this earth, and most accessible to those whose hearts are open to all the forms of God or Goddess.

Think about your relationship with God. How is this relationship established? God the Mother and God the Father, who are one, always listen to their children's prayers and thoughts. They can hear every sound that takes place on Mother Earth—every laugh or sigh or weeping. They are never too far away to listen to your heart. They are not far away at all. You never need fear that what they will hear is not sacred enough. Only when you think that God cannot hear or see you can disharmony come into your lives.

God is a state of being, and everyone is a child of God. The trouble is that you forget who you are. The mystic sees you all as the children of God, of an interfaith God who is so big that you can worship any god or goddess and your worship will be fully accepted.

Neem Karoli Baba, my guru, taught me how to speak to God the Formless. My gratitude goes to Baba for showing that the spirit within every one of us is the eternal essence of all religions. The truth of the interfaith path has always been. You just have to sit quietly and feel it.

"What is God?" I ask my Baba each day. It is not that I want to know; it is just that I love his answers. Today he said deep in my heart, "God just is." I loved that he said this. God just is! My teaching to you is to look for God within every human being you come across, to accept everyone, to have compassion for everyone, and to remember also your own perfection. "God just is," and he is everywhere you look.

True Love

It is time for you to experience the true power of love. To do this, dig deep into your heart, the storehouse of love.

Love conquers all things past and present and future. Never try to prove yourself to any other human being. Always trying to prove yourself right brings great heartache into the world. The spiritual seeker wants to be in the flow of this love—not to be right or wrong, not to be anything other than to be in love. When we are in that love, we feel no need to place anyone in the space of wrong. It is not another's religion that matters, or the form of God one worships, or one's sexual orientation. Love is the answer for all questions, and in the love of God we all are equal.

As others try to make themselves right, just send them love, whether they are near or far from you. This way you will always feel full rather than empty, because the storehouse of love is ever full.

The spiritual seeker wants only to be in the moment—the Mother's moment. Even those who are filled with fear about their lives can feel the Mother's love and the space of grace given to everyone. Ignorance of this love is a disease of the soul. But in truth, no seeker can be ignorant of this love. It lives and breathes inside of you as your essential nature, as the essential nature of every human being. Sit for a moment and feel the supreme Self within your being. It will make itself known in the quiet. It will remain veiled only if you want it to be veiled.

Live each day in a higher state of consciousness, and try to connect with all people on the level of love. The fastest and surest way to unveil the supreme Self is to serve and serve some more. This whole teaching is based on the sharing of love through service. When one serves another there is no egoism. How can there be room for ego if you are serving from the heart?

There are many knots in the heart that can only be untied by love. One by one allow these knots to be undone. You will know when this happens, because you will feel a special freedom in the moment. One day it comes to you. You get it! It takes you by surprise. All along the change has been happening subtly, and you may not even have noticed it until one day you do not react with anger as you would have before, you do not feel hurt as you would have before, and you are not as brash as you might have been before. The realization happens swiftly. Suddenly you are in love with all of life, and all of life is in love with you. As you feel a new love being born, you enter into the deep and simple wisdom in your heart of hearts.

Live to Serve

When you find your spiritual teacher or guru and fall in love as never before, your whole life takes on a new intensity. The feeling of love starts out slow but strong, and over the years it grows and grows and glows ever brighter. This love is a powerful wave of shakti that will sustain you all your life. When you are united in love with your guru, your feelings reach outward and touch all human sufferings. You want to seek help for the world, and through your love it is you who will ease the suffering of the many.

Pleasure and pain always alternate as the wheel of life and death continues to revolve around the ego and all the ego-thoughts of the limited mind. Without the limitation of the ego, the mind itself opens to the possibility of bliss. When the ego-mind begins to melt away, the heart will show the seeker how to be balanced in all conditions of pleasure and pain and how to wish all that is good for everyone else. The true Self beyond the ego knows neither anger nor pain nor grief nor sorrow. The Self knows only the moment and does not betray the moment by being a judge or jury. The Self knows only love.

When you care for others, everything that belongs to your small, personal interest begins to fade, and the desire to serve takes over. You do not want to serve for your own glory, for that would defeat the whole purpose.

When you serve others, you feel kindness and compassion growing in the heart. On the path of God and service, you never stop learning and growing. On the other hand, when you never think of another human being, painful conditions lodge in your heart. As long as the mind does not pay attention to the fullness of the heart, you will not understand the joy of serving God's children. But when the ego is set aside, the heart becomes full and able to feel the moment of love.

Now is the time to relax the concerns of your own life and serve with an open and full heart. Through the purifying shakti of service, you tap into the flow of God's love. You have no expectations but are happy to be filled always with this endless flow of love. When you love God with all your heart and soul, you begin to merge in God herself. In the divine height of love, all dualities disappear. There is no separation between the heart, the Self, the guru, and God. A devotee who knows this finds great happiness.

Lord Hanumanji is known as the god of service. He teaches how to serve from the very core of the heart. The key is to serve God with the purest devotion. To serve God with all your heart is to be freed from the misery and brittleness that comes to those who have forgotten the love of God.

No one is higher and no one is lower. Service is the great equalizer of all beings, those being served and those who are serving in the name of God. You will expand the horizons of your consciousness through serving others. Through service that is as selfless as Lord Hanumanji's, you will gain insight into the abundant spiritual potential that lives hidden in your unconscious.

It is time for you to become a giver. Know within how much you have to give to others and, of course, how much you have also to receive. Send all doubt away, and be in the moment of love. Love to love, and pay no heed to how the person to whom you are giving love responds.

When you are endowed with the unconditional love that allows your soul to be in tune with the universal soul, you can persevere through any obstacle. This power of devotion will bring you all the spiritual strength that you need to sustain your life with love and joy. As you serve, do not forget to practice meditation and spiritual inquiry. Because you serve, you will find that devotion to your God comes so much easier.

As you learn to serve others who are in need, the process of your spiritual growth opens you to living by spiritual intuition. While you have always lived with the senses that beckon you to your own gratification, you have not understood that God's light too has always been there within your heart of hearts.

The ego has no place when you are serving the poor or the sick. When you serve, the ego yields its place to an intuitional vision, and you begin to see into the very nature of your capabilities. You grow strong as you accept all peoples of the world, no matter how different they may appear. You begin to understand that universal love is the greatest of all loves. It is this unconditional love that lives in your heart and remains ever unstirred amid the troubles of the world. Service—taking care of others from the heart of hearts—is a way of coming ever closer to God. Remember this always: Service is the power of your silence in meditation transformed into action. Such service becomes worship that the Mother accepts with joy.

Your Responsibility

As you walk the spiritual path, God places a responsibility upon you to serve love to yourself and to others. You may ask, how does one serve love? The answer is not that difficult. To serve love is to keep your heart open no matter what. When you can do that, people will be able to feel love coming from you at all times.

On the other hand, if you choose to keep your heart closed, you waste an enormous amount of spiritual power, this divine shakti. Who gives you the right to waste this shakti? Do not forget that all of our shakti is given to us by the Mother, who feeds us and nourishes us. She holds you responsible to give this shakti away freely, and as you do so, it fills you more and more.

Take a moment to search your soul and discover that your relationship with God is based on unconditional love. There are no limitations, no boundaries, to that great love that is yours both to claim and to give away.

It is only when you forget the boundlessness that you allow tensions to enter into your life and take hold of your heart. Remember that darkness will always run before the beauty of love.

In the end, love is always the victor and always will be. In times of stress you must ask Mother Kali to take her sword of knowledge and split the tension with a swift stroke. She will do it as soon as you ask. She will give you the awareness to see through illusion. Then you must do whatever it takes to keep your heart open. It is not so hard. Simply pray, "Mother, touch my heart and keep it open and flowing." In this simple act of surrender you can take nourishment from her abundance.

The whole purpose of shakti is for you to feel divine love here on earth. Meditating longer and more deeply each day, you will learn to recognize your illusions. Leaving them aside, you will step into the reality of love.

When you wake to the dawn, ask for simple treasures: to notice the beauty of the rain and the sun and the moon and the stars, to be grateful for all that you have in your life, to be an instrument of God's grace.

To be an instrument of love will stir your heart like nothing else, because it is the most natural thing you can do. It is a simple way to live, being in love with life in the abundance of the now.

The great connection with abundance comes from serving others with full arms and fuller hearts.

The Mother, who is the love in your heart, is everywhere. She is in the sick and downtrodden, always there in the hearts of the poor and the lonely. Serve them and you serve her. It is an illusion to think that you do not have the responsibility to serve, or the ability. You can serve in your own way, and it is only a matter of finding your own way by living fully in your heart of hearts. The innermost essence of the heart is supreme love, understanding, and acceptance. Follow your heart, follow its call to responsibility, and it will lead you to joy.

Keeping It Simple

When you allow your spiritual essence to bloom, the scent of the heart is as fragrant as jasmine and rose, only it is deeper and comes through your very pores.

This transformation happens through meditation. First, you sit and feel quiet and still. If you do not feel the stillness, do not give up. Sitting while the mind goes in waves is only the first step. In this discipline you do not confront the thoughts but greet them with simple acknowledgement, without adding more thoughts.

As you prepare for your day, do not allow the obstacles in your mind to destroy the moment of simplicity. The ego puts those obstacles in your way. Pay no attention to them. Instead, be devoted to your God within the heart. There is nothing greater than devotion to destroy the obstacles. There is no mystery in how to live a full life of love and devotion. Just live in your spiritual essence. You were meant to be happy.

Keep life simple. Let go of what you do not need. Know that love is complete trust, and that love can nourish you in every way. Take into yourself the greatest amount of love that you can hold. Make enough space within your own being for the god or goddess of your tradition. Keep it simple and keep it real. That is enough: to live a simple life filled with God.

Only in simplicity can you feel a joy that would have you face any situation with a God-filled heart. You are the architect of your own destiny, and everything that you need is already in you. In simplicity you can recognize this.

The Mother cries out to you, "I am all existence, knowledge, and bliss. Know this and live in my heart forever." In the stillness of simplicity you can hear these words resound in your heart. Your Mother is like the beautiful jasmine flower, and you become the bee that never leaves it. Follow the sweet scent, and she will lead you to your true Self.

There is one thing that would keep you from the Mother, and that is pride. Spiritual pride is just as wrong as earthly pride. The Mother loves that which is done with the heart and not with the mind, so whether you are working, serving, praying, or meditating, always do so with humility and gratitude.

The Mother can be the foundation of all meditations on love. Ask her to bring you to her feet and fill you with her bliss. Religions may differ, yet truly the great gods and goddesses of all religions want to bring humanity to kindness and truth. God embraces all ways, and each path is a living reality of purity and love. Each presents itself with different words but the same message. The same love brings us all together. It is that simple, my chelas, if you let it be.

INTERLUDE

Durga Puja

DURGA PUJA

Each autumn, the ten days of Durga Puja are a special time of celebration. During this holy season we worship the Mother Kali on the first three nights, the gracious and generous Mother Laxmi on the next three, and the gentle Mother Saraswati on the last three. On these nine nights of Mother worship, become intoxicated, my chelas, with the love of guru and paramaguru. After the nine nights, the tenth day is a celebration of Mother Durga and the victory of the heart, which has conquered all negativity and darkness.

Feel the atmosphere of this special season and know that you are one with the Mother and that the Mother is one with you. Love can come toward you with the speed of light as you open your heart to acceptance.

On the first night at Kashi we ask the fierce but loving Mother Kali to destroy our negativity and to take from us all that which we do not need. As the dark Mother engages our minds and hearts, our whole being absorbs her teaching on how to live and how to die. In order to hear her voice, you need to have discipline. The black Mother is willing to spread open her arms and bring all of you to her nourishing breasts. Are you willing? What is stopping you? You were made to be happy.

Here at Kashi we do not fear death. Therefore we are so very alive. I welcome you all to change your lives. Do you want to? It's all about the cremation ground. Are you bold enough to lay your ego down on your own funeral pyre and let Mother Kali's flames consume that heavy load that you do not need? Can you let go of your fear?

I give you Kali. I have shown you the deepest secret. She is yours for a smile, for a word. All you need to do is ask, and she will come to you and be with you always.

On the middle three nights of Durga Puja we turn to Mother Laxmi, who is also known as Sri. Truly she is the most loved Goddess in all of India, for she graces us beyond comparison. She bids her children to ask her for the smallest and the largest blessings. Look toward her and receive her blessings of good fortune, prosperity, health, wisdom, and happiness in the abundance of the now.

Let us ask for just enough from her abundance to meet our own needs and then pray for her to be generous toward others.

I feel so bad for minds that remain crippled and tightly shut, unable to move toward the Mother's compassion and love. I see how such people get tangled up in anger and despair. Stay open, my chelas, and you will discover the beautiful you. Do not struggle with what other people think of you or your path. Love who you are in this wonderful moment. It is as simple as that. Understand that the essential nature of life is to love and to receive love. Use this time of Durga Puja to grow spiritually through the Mother Laxmi's grace, however you want or need to grow.

On the last three nights we worship the gentle Mother Saraswati and ask for spiritual knowledge and liberation.

She is the goddess of speech, music, and art—magnificently beautiful in her white sari. Her lovely face and figure are a joy to behold. But mostly what I'd like you to learn is the way she speaks. Not only with eloquence, but also with kindness and serenity. Do not let your own words take you from the moment. Do not look to hurt another human being. Let Saraswati's gentle power of creativity create your whole personality, and then you too will bring joy to the Mother herself.

Use these nights to find out who you are, first to your guru and then to yourself. When the mind chatters on, you cannot concentrate on who you are; yet, if you think with your heart, all your confusion and fear melt away in the light of the Self-knowledge that is Mother Saraswati's gift.

When you connect all the forms of Shakti to your own power of prayer and puja, you create an enormous amount of love for others. As we all love the form of God or Goddess on our own path, we open up to one another, and the interfaith teaching of love and service becomes a way of life. Accepting all ways of the hearts and souls of others opens your minds and hearts and gets your creative energy flowing, and then the flow never stops.

So, my chelas, during this Durga Puja, the consciousness of the Mother in her many forms blends into a single force for your benefit. At the end of the ten days, it will be time for all of you to put into action what you have learned. As this holy season comes to an end, remember that every end marks a new beginning. For us it is the start of a whole new year.

Always remember how much you are loved by the Mother and by your guru and paramaguru. It does not take a concentrated effort to understand this mystical love that never stops giving. The energy, or shakti, of this love centers itself in the core of your heart and then expands and expands. All who are around you can see and feel it. The flow of shakti, like the flow of the holy Ganga, never stops. It has always been with you, and now that you have cultivated your awareness of it, now that this shakti has awakened, you can keep your heart open and always be aware of your own divinity. From morning to evening and on to every next day, stay in the newness and wonder of it all.

These days of Durga Puja change everything for the better for all who come closer and closer to living in a spirit of worship. It is you yourselves who must tend the shrine of the heart and keep it an inner place of worship and joy. Waves and waves of bliss wash over you as you live in the Mother's light. Pure awareness is yours as you live your life in her.

PART FOUR
The Goal

Self-Knowledge

Know yourself. There is a vastness in meditation that stretches the heart to reveal the divine presence within you. Do not turn away even if the urge to turn away is there. The human mind is limited, but true knowledge and wisdom grow in the higher mind that seeks guidance from the heart. When the intellect is purified through meditation, drifting thoughts no longer take hold and take root. You will know that which is permanent within you. Face this, your divine Self, and know for sure that you are a part of God—and not apart from God.

Ordinarily you think you exist in the world of time and space, and you feel an inner hunger. This great hunger is in fact to become one with God, but most of the time you think that this hunger is starving for things of the world. You have forgotten that the God-mind in you is your essential nature, beyond the things of the world and the mind. If you look closely within yourself and notice when you are truly the happiest, you will recognize that it is God that you really hunger for.

It is time to discover your timeless immortality. Your human body is finite, yet you hunger for infinity. Everything perishes, yet you hunger for the imperishable. Look deeply and see that your true goal is to taste the nectar of the divine Self. Here all illusions are transcended.

The lower ego-self is limited, but the higher God-self has no boundaries. Meditation lifts the veil of ignorance. Allow your own breath to lead you to the present moment, the timeless moment where you will feel how ancient you are and will know the ancient wisdom you possess. The light of the Self is seen by the yogi who meditates daily and sees the end of duality. This is the light in which you see God in all, and all in God. When this light is known, then all is known.

All that is not permanent will perish while the Self goes on and on. The Self is eternal; neither life nor time can touch it.

You can discover your own timelessness and your own holiness here and now. Whenever you sit, either in the presence of a holy person or the gods and goddesses in the shrine, the silence that comes to you regenerates your being. In this silence all duality ceases to be, and truth is felt and experienced. When you and your truth become one, you can literally taste God.

If you could close your eyes right now and get in touch with the perfection of your soul, you would feel that perfection for a fleeting moment in time and space. You have wandered through lifetimes in different bodies throughout time, and as long as you have not found the divine Self within, you have not found fulfillment. If you continue to follow the same old path, pursuing gratification of mind, emotions, and senses, will you find fulfillment in this life?

Now is the moment to know that you can choose fulfillment by serving humanity. Be thrilled to have received a body in which to work out your existing karma. This is a first step on the road to perfection.

Everything in life can bring you to God if you let it. God loves to love; allow yourself to receive that love. Every such moment has a newness that is yours to contemplate. This state of acceptance is where heaven meets with earth, and surely this is true. Experience this opening of your heart.

No seeking. No searching. Just being who you are. Just being the divine Self.

The Divine Presence

Meditate on God's permanence, and when you emerge from meditation, you will feel that you have awakened from the slumber you have been living in. Now look around you with awareness and see in your own surroundings colors that you have not noticed before. Take in the wonder. Do not let yourself be confused any longer, but know that the law of karma unfolds its secret to those who are aware: the secret is that you have the freedom of choice in every given moment.

As you search for the divine Self, you will find that you always were in touch with the Self. When you become aware of your life, your breath, and your heart in this way, you benefit from the powerful love of God flowing into you. You will be able to recognize it. Meditation brings awareness of the Self, and this awareness brings spiritual bliss. The yogis speak of total wakefulness in *samadhi,* in the state of oneness with God.

The highest level of consciousness becomes available to you as the mind slows down and the heart opens wide. It is your soul's destiny to be in the joy of God all your life. Becoming your highest Self is your soul's destiny.

There is a divine light shining in your heart at every moment. Surrender to this light, which is yours, which has always been yours, and let this great light flood your whole being. Feel the waves of its love sweep over you and touch you at every part of your being.

Feel peace. A state of permanent peace brings freedom from limitation and pain. There is wisdom in peace, and the path of spiritual wisdom is a holy path. Helping others is even more holy. The moment you are attuned to your inner peace, you become an inspiration for others to find peace in themselves. The moment you are freed from your own pain, you can be available to serve others who have pain. Thus you bring love and more love to this earth of ours.

Meaning and Clarity

There is nothing in you that is meaningless. Everything you do, every breath you take, short or long, can mean something. You only need to be aware. Your heart is the space where your higher God-self can answer the question, "What does life mean?"

Meaningful answers can come only from yourself, from the deepest part of your being. A moment of insight can help you come to terms with all the pain and grief in the world. By being in your heart, you can bring love to the world. Even if you help just a little bit, that little bit adds up.

Becoming holy does not mean you have to be holy in another's eyes, only in your own. So, the real question to ask, of course, is the very simple, "Who am I?" The Self should never be identified with the mental things that come up as the ego begins to die. The Self, though not separate from anything, has nothing to do with the ego, except that the ego tries to cover it with its attachments. Ask the Mother to use her divine weapons to slay the ego and bring you to freedom from doubt and pain. As your meditation becomes deeper and deeper, there are steps of wisdom that you climb. Your increasing wisdom connects you to all that is and all that ever was. As understanding takes root in this lifetime, it will remain throughout all lifetimes. Through this awareness the clouds are brushed away, and the higher mind becomes clear.

Until then, many aspects of shakti are hidden in everyone but usually cannot be seen directly. Your unconscious is filled with this shakti, this power, which lies waiting to be used. You need only get rid of the surrounding clouds to enter the clear sky of shakti. Every once in a while you get a glimpse of the clarity within and begin to experience the glory of a spiritual path. You do not have to—and should not have to—depend on outer conditions to experience happiness.

There is happiness in the moment if you can be quiet enough to feel the joy of the clear sky of shakti. A blissful expansion of the Self reaches the surface of the heart as you sit in meditation. After a while, you can live this expansion in your world and never have the feeling of separation. There comes a spontaneous love that cannot be hidden from yourself or from others. The simple truth is that everything in life is created by God to be enjoyed by the human heart. When you give thanks for your life and for the small things in life, the big things will come and gratitude will grace the innermost part of your being. "Who am I?" Practice this spiritual inquiry, and you will find a wonderful place in the universe where you can be at all times. You will find that you are the joy of your own heart. Your heart is the joy of your God and Goddess. Your life, if lived in God, becomes meaningful and joyous.

Your Own Perfection

Whenever the mind is not focused, it is confused. Throughout time humans have been running after this or that, have tried to become this or that. Yet they do not know that they are already perfect in the eyes of God.

When you stop pursuing or seeking you will find that which you already have, that which you already are. Think of this moment only and of the beauty of loving God. Be grateful—actively so—and bring that gratitude into every movement of mind and body. There is grace coming to you at all times, and when grace comes, there can be no conflict. Do not deviate into the past, but stay in the vitality of the moment.

Once your heart is open, you begin to see your own perfection and the perfection in everything and everyone. You begin to relate to people in a sacred way. You are always in a state of love. You begin to know how timeless you are, how much you are loved, and how capable you are of being loved. Never underestimate your own power of love, for the power of love is the most powerful of all shaktis.

Then why is there so much trouble in this world of ours? The answer is so simple: trouble comes when we forget our perfection. So many do not acknowledge the perfection within themselves. Find this truth in yourself by sitting each day and meditating. Just to discover in meditation that you are not separate from God or guru brings happiness to the heart.

The Mother's great love is in you, abiding deep in the inner places of God. This universe is the divine vision of the Divine Mother, and you are a part of that divine vision. If your personal spiritual path is one of self-acceptance, it will also be a path of bliss and joy.

We are all perfect when we allow love to reveal our perfection. Each time we sit in meditation, we enter that holy place in the heart. Sacredness is ever there, in you and in me. You—we—are the perfection of God's creation. You can feel this as you breathe in and out of your heart. Feel the oneness of this moment, and keep the oneness with you. Be in the oneness all this day as you go about. It is only a matter of knowing, of being in the knowing.

Everything is full and empty at the same time. As long as you live in the present moment, the emptiness and the fullness are truly one, and your own experience of the moment is the only truth you know. To attain the absolute atman (the supreme Self, which is God), you must be in the moment twenty-four hours a day. Then day and night and time all disappear into timeless bliss. The uninterrupted bliss of God belongs to and can be felt by every seeker of God.

Expanding

Me and *mine*—once you give up those words, you become free to say God's words. This brings you closer to your heart of hearts, closer to living in the moment, which has the vibration of perfection. This perfection is none other than God the Mother and God the Father.

Perfection goes on forever and ever, even though you've thought that it eluded you lifetime after lifetime. Then one lifetime you get it all! Perfection greets you, and you know that it was never absent. Not ever.

Make that moment happen. Come into the spaceless, timeless place of love in your heart. This place is independent of time and space, yet in it you always have a choice—every moment—to live your life in the beauty of God, or else to complain and be unhappy.

Gratefulness always reveals the happiness within. Be grateful because you are whole and holy. Know your holiness this moment. Know that there is no separation between you, your guru, and God. Feel the power of this divine connection, and you will know that denial of God in your life is a waste of shakti.

The road to harmony lies within yourself. The road to perfection lies within yourself. Shakti lies within yourself, and when you can recognize your own God-power, you become awake and aware.

It is very simple. On your spiritual journey you are given the ability to learn what is needed when it is needed. The Mother is there in the heart so you can be in touch with her at any moment. As she calls you to her, you enter into a relationship with her, and she allows you to become more aware of who you are.

Attaining Tranquility

As you meditate, some thoughts come to an end and others begin. This is natural. Acknowledge that, but keep breathing with awareness. You will come to know the ancient wisdom of the breath.

The sleeping heart wakes up to the sound of deep breathing. The Ganga floods the heart as it wakes up to life. Your thoughts are part of you, so do not place them in a space that you deem negative. Ordinary thoughts are just words that go around and around in your head. Heart thoughts come from feeling the love of God. Between the thoughts, between the tiny gaps, is the pure space where you can feel the present moment that fills you with light. As you live in the moment, you live beyond thought.

The Divine Mother causes such a seeker to be serene and filled with love. All disquiet of the soul is relieved. You know beyond words and thoughts that you are one with infinity. The soul soars to its cosmic height as you live your life with awareness and love. Feel the tranquility of the soul in yourself and in everyone.

Spiritual Freedom

When you are in contact with the sweetness of your own divine Self, you are in contact with the universal Self that is God. Whenever you go toward love, you are going toward the Mother. When you truly meditate on the heart of love within you, the supreme consciousness arises from Mother Kali's fire of awareness. Thus you attain complete victory over the dark side of the mind and come into the light of your God-heart. Infinite freedom is yours.

Your unconscious mind becomes detached from worldly desires, and this detachment rises up into the conscious actions of your day. With good works that bring joy to others, you can burn up the seeds of karma that you carry within you. To attain liberation while yet alive is to live a full, God-centered life that can benefit everyone on Earth.

To attain your dream of liberation, you have to know that you are already liberated and only have to remove the clouds of illusion that hide the core of love that you are and always have been. When you understand this only a little, illusion begins to disappear. Do not allow your vision of God to be deluded by maya. Maya is difficult to consume, yet with devotion there is nothing that is too difficult. Therefore, become firmly rooted on the path of devotion and love.

When delusion is gone, duality will soon be gone as well. When you say to the God of your choice that you will do her or his bidding, then you are prepared to become one with that God.

The teachings of Tantra are about the merging of God and seeker, a merging beyond the thoughts of the human mind. This merging is of the heart. Victory and happiness belong to the seeker who is ready to merge with God. There is triumph in the heart of the Mother as her child becomes one with her being.

Grace and divinity become personified when the seeker surrenders to God. As surrender becomes part of one's life, there is great relief in the heart. To have all one's doubts dissolve is pure bliss. The soul, joined with God, is at peace in this lifetime. The bliss of the end can be brought to the life of the now. Like a bright light, the essence of God drips into the heart of the seeker, who is set free of the bonds of life and death.

The seeker then lives for the glory of God and the well-being of humanity. One who attains the peace of freedom wants this peace for others and lives to bring others to God.

Opening the Heart to Oneness

There comes a moment when, through the subtle heart of meditation, so much becomes clear: you begin to see things as oneness instead of as duality. Through the silent power of this inner experience, the heart transcends the mind. As the mind is controlled, you will begin to discover that you are soaring beyond its worldly illusions—illusions that the mind creates.

As you evolve spiritually, you will discover that you are not the limited personality that you always thought you were. As you breathe into your chest and awaken your heart, you begin to feel the soul. Getting to know your soul is about being really quiet, but that is not enough. This individual soul, the jivatman, must then be merged into the universal atman, or God-Self. The atman is pure oneness: one life that vibrates with joy in all beings. You cannot feel this oneness unless the heart is open always.

When the heart is open, you are without borders or lines; you are free. It is a matter of allowing the lower mind to be consumed by the God-mind that you always knew was in you, hidden but there, and in this way you will come to abide in the divine Self.

The divine Self is the oneness that is all of ours to enjoy. It is the great spiritual strength in everyone. One who lives in the knowledge of the oneness has gained mastery over the senses and is able to control anger, hatred, and egoism. The oneness is so vast that there are no words to describe it. In fact, there are no words. There is only oneness. It is something you feel in the core of your being. It *is* the core of your being, older than existence itself.

Don't think, don't get lost in words, just go straight to your heart and try to feel the oneness. Take this first step, and take it over and over until the darkness of not-knowing begins to dissolve in the light of the opening heart. It is the Mother's shakti that brings you the energy of wisdom, and this gift of wisdom comes easily to one with an open heart.

You were born to attain God-consciousness and to bring this consciousness to the world. In your daily life you will live to discover the beauty of God within you and within all who live upon the Earth. As you recognize the love of God and Goddess shining ever brighter, you will become an inspiration for everyone.

The Experience of Now

The purpose of spiritual teaching is to remind you of what you already know. This knowing comes from deep within. You can feel it the most when you are silent in meditation. This knowing makes itself known to you, and through it you begin to gain insight into your life and the lives of others. You begin to understand your own power. You begin to understand who you truly are.

We can live fully only in the present moment. Yesterday has already died and tomorrow has yet to be. Today is the only day there is. Therefore, never be clouded by the conflict of past memories or future fears.

If you try to prepare for tomorrow, you will find out fast enough that tomorrow never comes. Your dreams come true with the reality of the now. Attend to the experience of this moment, and experience the bliss of the now. Breathe in this moment and feel the divine wisdom in your heart. Do not look for explanations of the now. Instead, feel the love. Let the mind rest in the beauty of the now, and know that all you can learn in your life is the experience of the now.

Every once in a while you experience a great bliss. Every once in a while you have full understanding of the oneness. Unfortunately this does not happen often enough. Too often you feel unfulfilled, even though fulfillment is just a breath away. You keep going back and reliving the past. You dwell on the mistakes you made. Or maybe you avoid thinking of the mistakes you made and only talk of the good old days. Either way, you stop yourself from living in the moment. The now becomes fainter and fainter if you do not learn how to live in its eternal newness.

The now is all we have, and we must make the most of it. Once we let go of past experiences, or at least learn from them, then the indescribable light of the now overpowers all the darkness of past events. Once we let go of our fears of what the future may bring, then the light of the now overpowers the darkness of our fears.

Draw your God-consciousness from the depth of your soul and swim in the Mother's love—now! Feel the moment, drink in the moment, be the moment, and love the moment—now!

Meditate on your third eye and see the light of the now. Know that you are part of this light. This third eye is the guru chakra, because guidance dwells in its holy light. Direct your attention there and think of this light, of nothing but this light, and be in the now.

Let us start with this moment. You are being reminded to live in this beautiful moment of reality. The teacher or guru can only point the way to inner peace and happiness; it is you who have to decide to take the chance on loving the moment with all your heart and soul.

Awakening to the Inner Light

Deep within you is a great hunger to find your own Self, the Self that is unaffected by the pleasures and pains of life, the Self that is untouched by the limits of time and space, the Self that is one with God.

This inner Self is ever present but manages to remain hidden, masked by self-doubt and feelings of unworthiness. It is masked by the cravings for all that you feel missing from your life. Because most human actions belong to the world of desires, you wander to and fro, seeking, ever seeking that which you think will bring you happiness. Lifetime after lifetime you continue along the same path of desire and attachment, and you always come to the same endings.

The truth is that you have forgotten that your true desire is only for God, and if you look closely enough you will discover that longing in the depth of your heart. You will find that your goals lie not in worldly achievement, for such satisfaction comes and goes, but that the supreme goal is to know the shining Self at the core of your soul.

Behind the ever-changing world of duality, there is a reality which is the permanent state. The guru teaches that the Self is immortal, ageless, deathless, and everlasting.

Now is the time to taste and feel the love deep in your heart, the love that is the Self. This is the divine reality behind all the different forms of God. The many forms that God takes always lead to the formless God, the silent Mother, the still heart. God never changes and is always the same, always unconditional. Look deeply behind all forms and feel the permanence of God.

The divine Self is pure consciousness and wisdom. Like a great light that never begins and never ends, it shines by itself. It never needs another light to reveal it, but sees by its own light. The Self lives on and on, never changing. When you meditate every day, you begin to get glimpses of the Self, the atman. It can be known by its own brightness.

As you begin to realize your own divinity, your life becomes more and more fulfilled. The essence of completeness is the great love that is in you. If you can see this love within as the great light of Lord Shiva when you close your eyes, then eventually you will feel yourself established in the middle of this light. Whatever you need is in this light, and the more you can live in the light, the vision of divine love will bring you everything you ever wanted or needed.

The mistaken need to create more and more karma arises because you have not learned from your past actions; this simply melts away. From now on your spiritual heart knows exactly what to do in each circumstance. When you allow the light of God to burn steady in your spiritual heart and always feel the divine passion, you will keep your life balanced and your heart open in bliss.

Throughout the day take a moment now and then to look toward your third eye and feel the great orb of the sun filling you with the sound of OM, and in its sacred vibration love to love and enjoy your life. I cannot say it enough: *you are the divinity that you seek.*

Everything else is just a covering—the intellect, the ego, the mind, the body. And yet you must keep the body healthy and strong. The body houses the individual soul, the jivatman, throughout each lifetime. Within and beyond the jivatman, the light of the unchanging, blissful Self ever shines.

Your small "I" is the little ego, born of separation and not-knowing. Service cleanses the heart and helps to get rid of this small "I"; it helps you to feel the great beauty of the large "I," the one that merges with *paramatman,* the universal Self. This is the supreme "I" that makes you complete. This supreme "I" has a power, called shakti, which resides in everyone as Kundalini, the Mother's essential energy that you begin to feel in spiritual life. Kundalini is always rising and falling, not unlike the breath, once you are made aware.

As long as you identify only with the body, you will never realize the fullness of the spirit, which you truly are. When your small mind thinks that you are only this flesh, this is bondage. The physical body is only something lent to us while we are on this Earth. It comes and goes, comes and goes. The spirit always is. When attachment begins to leave you, you grow closer to the one great spirit that we all share. This spirit, or God, is beyond time, space, mind, and body. Yet the gods and goddesses can be reached at any given moment. Be fearless in your pursuit of God in form and God the formless. Keep your mind steady with the image of your own God or path.

Keep very still, and reach into your heart. Go past the clouds of your senses. Do not let yourself be tormented by the doubting mind. If doubt arises, sing and chant to God the Mother and feel her near you. Devotion will give you the shakti to go on. Fight against your own sense of unworthiness by remembering that you are created in the divine image. End the duality in your heart, and you will feel the freedom of non-judgment. There may be imperfection in the individual soul, but the Self is perfect. The Self is perfect oneness.

A way to get past the clouds of illusion is through serving those in need. When you truly serve, you learn never to judge but to see the beauty in others. When you bow to that beauty in your heart of hearts, soon everything will be the same, internally and externally. You will know the Self in yourself and recognize that same Self in others. Then everything will be united in the miracle of divine love.

If you can bow before the majesty of the Self in your own heart, you bow also before the majesty of that same divine Self in others. You will learn, ever so clearly, that serving and taking care of the poor and sick and elderly and homeless brings you closer to the God-self within your own being. Like meditation, service free of ego is a path to enlightenment. Serving others brings harmony in your life.

You will know when your will runs parallel to the will of God, because you will be one who promotes happiness in others. You will adapt to all conditions in your life and to the different kinds of people who come your way. With every breath let your heart expand more and more, and allow each day to bring forth new visions of serving others. When you serve them, you help yourself, so let each day unfold with the great spiritual teachings born of service.

Get used to listening to others before you speak. In this way you will become adept at listening to your heart thoughts, and that will make it easier for you to reach in and find the Self. The more you are in touch with the Self, the more your life is filled with God and the more you become aware of who you truly are.

Turn the mind toward the Self. Meditate on the Self. It is like a vessel filled with *soma*, the nectar of the gods. It can be felt in the gap in between two thoughts. It is that moment of stillness that brings you great peace. As you practice meditation, the mind will continue to flow after the gap between two thoughts. Only it will flow like a beautiful river, and thoughts will gradually be put to rest longer and longer.

In this profound peace you are never alone: the Mother is with you every day of your life. As the lower mind begins to melt in the fire of the Mother's love, the higher mind wakes up to the higher awareness of the Self. The Self is always there for you to tune in to. Let the quiet touch you. The Mother is the quiet. The Mother is the silence. The Mother is always with you. Is the Mother any different from the Self?

Commit yourselves to finding your true Self. You will find the teaching and the guidance at the feet of your teacher or guru, who learned it at the feet of the paramaguru, and so on, in a great lineage of holy men and women.

This knowledge of the Self is that wisdom that you already know. You need only to remove the covering of not-knowing to discover it there, ever shining. Let this lifetime be the one in which you awaken to the inner light. It lies within your power to awaken to the bliss of God. Through meditation and service you can come to your own essential nature. Through meditation and service you can discover the timeless joy of the immortal Self.

The Self Is Love

The heart of God is in everyone. No matter who you are, you carry within your being the heart—the essence—of God. You only need to sit quietly and listen to the God that lives in your heart as a deep well of wisdom and knowledge.

There is no breath without this divine reality, no life or movement. She dwells there in the heart as your true inner being, and when you are through with this body, she still is. The body, mind, and senses do not affect the God of your heart, which is your divine essence. This is the Self, the atman—and the Self is detached and ever free. Yet, it is wherever you go as you sit and yearn for the gift of God's love.

A hindrance to recognizing your true being is to think that you are alone. Such a feeling arises when worldly thoughts or painful thoughts come up. Mental illusions come to those who forget to put in the time to meditate on the heart, but those who go deeper and deeper into the heart find it ever easier to enter into this sacred space of the Self. Otherwise, you think that you are the body and the senses. The fact is, the Self is beyond time and space. There is no gender in the Self; there is no right or wrong religion; there is only a great and wonderful feast of love.

If you were to climb the highest mountain and look toward the great sky, you could not feel more peaceful or expansive than if you just closed your eyes and felt God all around you and in you. Through meditation you climb to the highest heights of mysticism. Through the understanding born of meditation you begin to distinguish reality from illusion. There is no illusion in love: love can remove any darkness in the world. The sweetness of God is always with you. You only have to be quiet enough to feel it and hear it and *be* it.

The Self cannot burn or be pierced or hurt in any way. Water cannot drown it, nor can it be torn. The Self is immovable and eternal, omnipresent and all-pervading. The Self is the foundation of everything. There is nothing you can do to make the Self go away. It always was, always will be, and always *is*.

You only have to take a moment to find the love within your own being to understand the nature of the pure Self in you and in everyone else. *Behold the Self:* your divinity waits to be acknowledged. The goal of life is to manifest this divinity in all your actions and deeds. Love others as you would want to be loved, and the Self will reveal itself. Find the place in you where you can recognize you, and you will understand that this is the divine Self.

The lamp of divine love burns always inside of you. Do not put out the flame with feelings of anger or depression. The beauty of the Self lights up this day and every day. Look at the trees holding up the sky; look at the flowers smiling at you. If you look, you will see. Look at the beauty of the Self. You are that beauty, whose light can never fade.

The sweetness of the Self is always yours to experience. It can end all the sorrows of anger you might feel. When there is thunder in the sky, you know that it will not last very long; soon the sun will be out again. When you feel the thunder rumbling through you in the form of anger, you must know in your heart that soon you will feel love again. What if you went right to the feeling of love and skipped the anger?

Be a hero to yourself this day and stop anger before you have a chance to react. Be constant in your meditation on love, and leave no room for anger. Attain the victory of discipline. Attain the victory of love.

In the Silence

How does one escape the outer chaos of the world and the inner chaos of the mind? What great wisdom can bring you to harmony? You need to bring the mind to its true condition, which is to dwell in the God-stillness of the heart. Therefore the wisdom that you seek is in the complete harmony of the mind and heart. This harmony is in yourself and can be found in meditation. When the mind and heart are in complete harmony, then there is no more chaos outside to intrude on your thoughts.

When the mind is not in chaos, the yogic body grows serene, and when the yogic body is content, it resonates with the stillness of samadhi

. The heart of the yogi can be renewed in the silence of the teacher's and God's unconditional love. Your responsibility to your own heart is to come to God-stillness.

The heart deteriorates when it is not filled with the ocean of God's love. If you feel empty inside, you know the agony of being apart from God. It is so sweet to love God with all your heart and soul. Give up what you do not need, whatever gets in your way, so you can fill up with the love of God the Mother and God the Father.

What you are in the moment begins to reveal itself. Gratitude is the light that shines forth and brings you back to all that you seek. To understand the silence in your heart is to be reminded of your deep relationship with God. Listen to your heartbeat within the cave of the heart. God will reveal herself. There is no reality in external chaos.

Between your thoughts stands the silence. When you meet that silence so deep in your heart, the world is drowned out. This silent truth of the heart holds the mind still and sets the soul free. This silence is the divine presence in us all. You literally sink into the silent heart of the Mother and are held by her warm and wonderful arms. The smokescreen of maya is cleared away as you feel the wonderment of the still moment. There is no way to describe it, and you can put whatever name to it that you wish.

We all have the habit of putting long sentences between us and our silence, but the best way to look at God's gift of herself is to say nothing at all. Just as you see the sunrise or a star falling in the early hours of dawn, only feel silent thanks for the moment. There is no "me" or "mine" in these events. There is only love—a love so pure that there is no need for words.

Hidden deep in your heart is a language of love so ancient that every now and then, without words, you understand another's heart. It is the Mother who speaks in the whisper of a flower growing. Do not lose the moment; do not lose one moment of loving and being loved. Once you have been touched by the silence, growth happens at a quicker pace. It is as if you are about to ripen on the vine and the Mother will allow you to taste your own great joy.

All that you do not need will fall away, and you will rejoice. As you live in the silence and bring it to the world in all your actions, your heart will merge with all hearts as one.

Om Tat Sat

Every time you say the word OM, as in a mantra before the name of God, you are invoking the Supreme Being. As you chant the holy words OM TAT SAT, you are remembering that all is one and that the One is in all. OM TAT SAT means "That which is That"—the truth or reality that is God. Thus by remembering this great mantra of God and Goddess throughout the day, you will not let your mind get in the way of your natural spirit of love. You will live every day loving God and knowing that God loves you. Such a simple thing to do.

I put this thought in your mind: invoke the name of God all this day. Set fire to your heart and feel the passionate warmth of love for God. All darkness will perish in this internal fire of the heart. The attachments that have woven a whole blanket of illusion will go up in flames.

At no time be comfortable with your limits. Expand, expand, expand. Transcend maya and realize the Self as the ocean of bliss: OM TAT SAT, OM TAT SAT, OM TAT SAT.

When the dreamer in the chamber of your heart is awakened to loving others and serving in the name of God, you will be awakened to the divine vision of yourself in the fullness of love for God and unbounded compassion for others. In the quiet of the dawn and throughout the day and into the night, the awakened one repeats the name of God all the time while treading the path of love and compassion. Know that you are the awakened one, just being yourself—your true Self—in this eternal moment of perfection.

175

The Mother's Prayer

O Mother of the Universe, protect my children with your deep love, and reveal your existence in their lives.

Manifest your compassion, wipe out their fears, and let them hear the sound of your voice this day.

Mother Kali, slay their thoughts of negativity and in their stead place loving thoughts and kindness of heart and awareness of soul.

Let my children never doubt their ability to love and to be loved, and grant them the strength of love.

Manifest in their hearts your wise ways, my beautiful black Mother Kali, and let my children know their own beauty.

Devour their false feelings of unworthiness, and teach them their purity.

Take away their anger and fear, that they may be filled full with spiritual joy. Teach them their purity, my beautiful black Mother Kali.

O you who are time, the great devourer, and the hungry devourer of time, reveal to my children the great harmony of life and death, and melt their egos in your fire's flames, that their small selves, separate no more, may merge in your universal Self.

Let them know you who are the oneness of all, and show them that all is in the oneness.

Let this day be the turning point, when their journey of the spirit becomes filled with your wisdom.

Protect them in the East, protect them in the West, protect them in the South, protect them in the North, in the heavens, and on the Earth.

You, who are the granter of all grace, allow my children this very day to see their lives as grace.

About the Author

Ma Jaya Sati Bhagavati (1940-2012) was a spiritual teacher, mystic, and visionary. She taught that divinity is ultimately beyond words and without form, yet manifests in countless ways to lead us to liberation. All paths of love can lead to spiritual awakening.

Ma Jaya's accomplishments include founding an interfaith community called Kashi Ashram; developing Kali Natha Yoga, a modern system drawn from ancient roots; guiding service projects in India, Uganda, and the US; working to end religious prejudice; supporting the LGBTQ community; overseeing a K-12 school; founding a model community for low-income seniors; and creating a large body of sacred art.

Born into a Jewish family in 1940, Ma Jaya grew up in a cellar apartment in Brighton Beach, Brooklyn, a short walk from the ocean and the famous Coney Island Boardwalk. As a young girl, she found love and solace among the homeless people who lived under the Boardwalk. Welcoming her, they taught her many lessons about life, especially, "There are no throwaway people." She grew up to dedicate her life to humanity.

At a weight loss class in 1972, she learned a simple yogic breath that would ultimately bring about her spiritual enlightenment. Her personal spiritual journey moved quickly and, at times, chaotically. As a modern urban woman, she tried to live a normal life and raise a family; at the same time, as a person of rare spiritual gifts, she daily opened to a series of mystical visions and experiences. She had experiences first of Jesus Christ, then of Shri Bhagawan Nityananda of Ganeshpuri, and eventually her guru, Shri Neem Karoli Baba. As early as 1973, she began to "teach all ways," as Christ had instructed her to do. She gave a contemporary voice to the great truths that underlie all spiritual paths.

She offered the example of a spiritual life alive with love, faith, creativity, service, and the rituals of many traditions. Emphasizing individual spiritual growth, she taught seekers at all levels and never asked her students to follow any particular set of doctrines or beliefs. Or, as she often said, "This is not a religion!" She encouraged her students to use her teachings within their own faiths or traditions, and to practice kindness.

Ma Jaya began to teach yoga and breath practices in 1973. In 2000 she began to share her yoga teachings more deeply and gave them the name Kali Natha Yoga. Her teachings on karma formed the basis for her book *The 11 Karmic Spaces: Choosing Freedom from the Patterns that Bind You*, which won a gold medal from the Independent Publishers' Association. Another book, *First Breath, Last Breath*, offers both inspiration and advice for those who study the practice of pranayama.

In 1976, Ma Jaya moved to Florida and founded Kashi Ashram, a spiritual community that embraces all religious and spiritual paths, where her students continue to teach and serve in her name.

About the Editor

Devadatta Kali (David Nelson) began his training in Hindu thought and practice in 1966 at the Vedanta Society of Southern California in Hollywood, under the guidance of Swami Prabhavananda, from whom he received initiation in 1969. In 1993 Devadatta first came into the presence of Ma Jaya Sati Bhagavati at the Parliament of the World's Religions in Chicago. After a personal introduction in New York the following year, he became associated with her ashram in Los Angeles, which marked the beginning of a long period of spiritual guidance and service.

In 1997, after a twenty-one-year professional career devoted to the international promotion and production of classical music recordings, Devadatta became increasingly active as a translator, writer, and lecturer on Hindu spirituality, with an emphasis on Upanishadic and Tantric teaching. He has contributed many articles to popular and scholarly publications in the United States and India and has spoken frequently at temples, churches, colleges, and interfaith conferences throughout Southern California.

Devadatta, who lives in Santa Barbara, is the author of *In Praise of the Goddess: The Devimahatmya and Its Meaning* (2003), *The Veiling Brilliance: A Journey to the Goddess* (2006), *Svetasvataropanisad: The Knowledge That Liberates* (2011), *Songs of Illumination: The Mystical Verse of Abhinavagupta* (2013), and *Managing the Mind: A Commonsense Guide to Patanjali's Yogasutra* (2015).

CPSIA information can be obtained
at www.ICGtesting.com
Printed in the USA
FSOW02n1927261017
40181FS